ZAHA HADID
Form in Motion

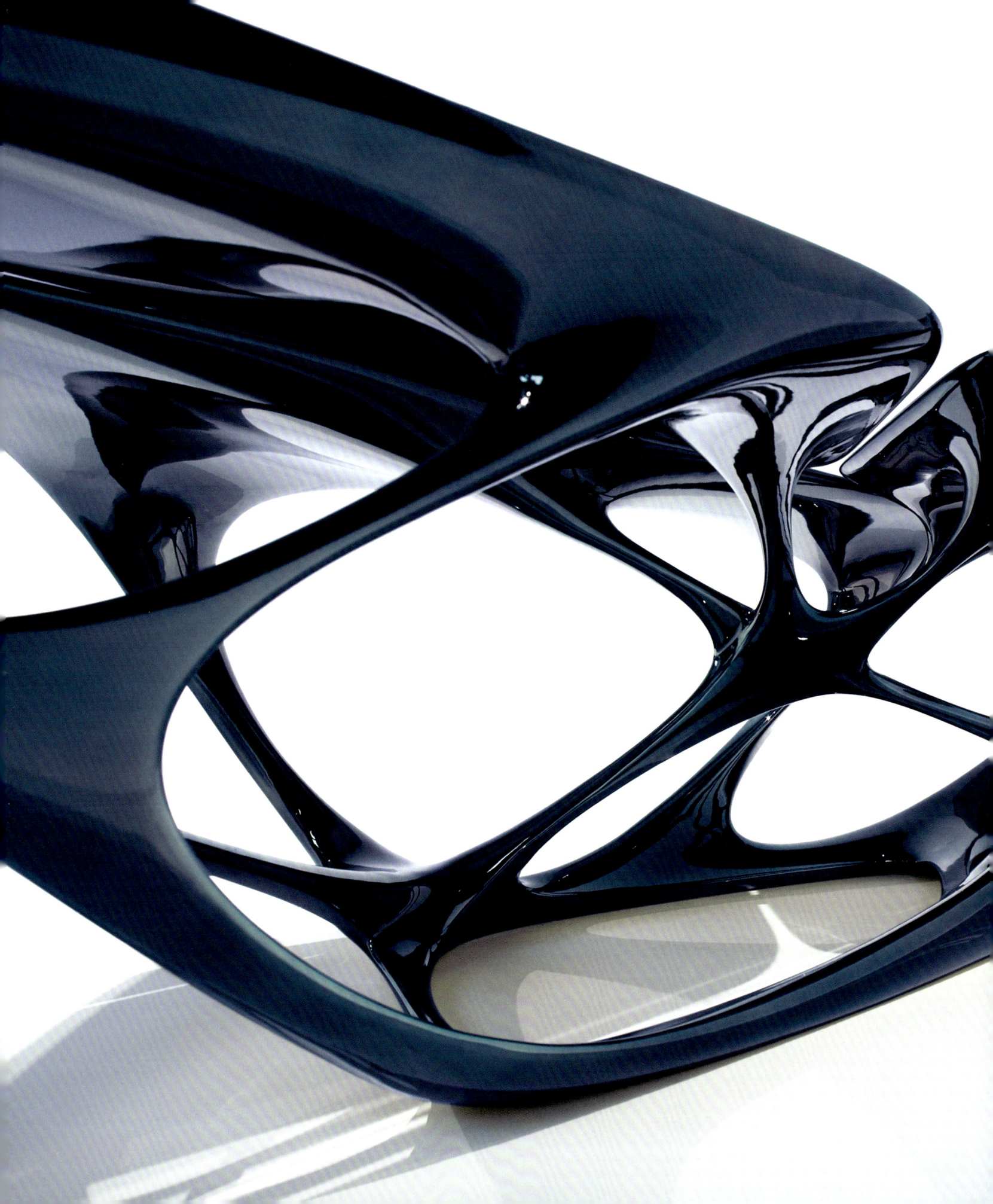

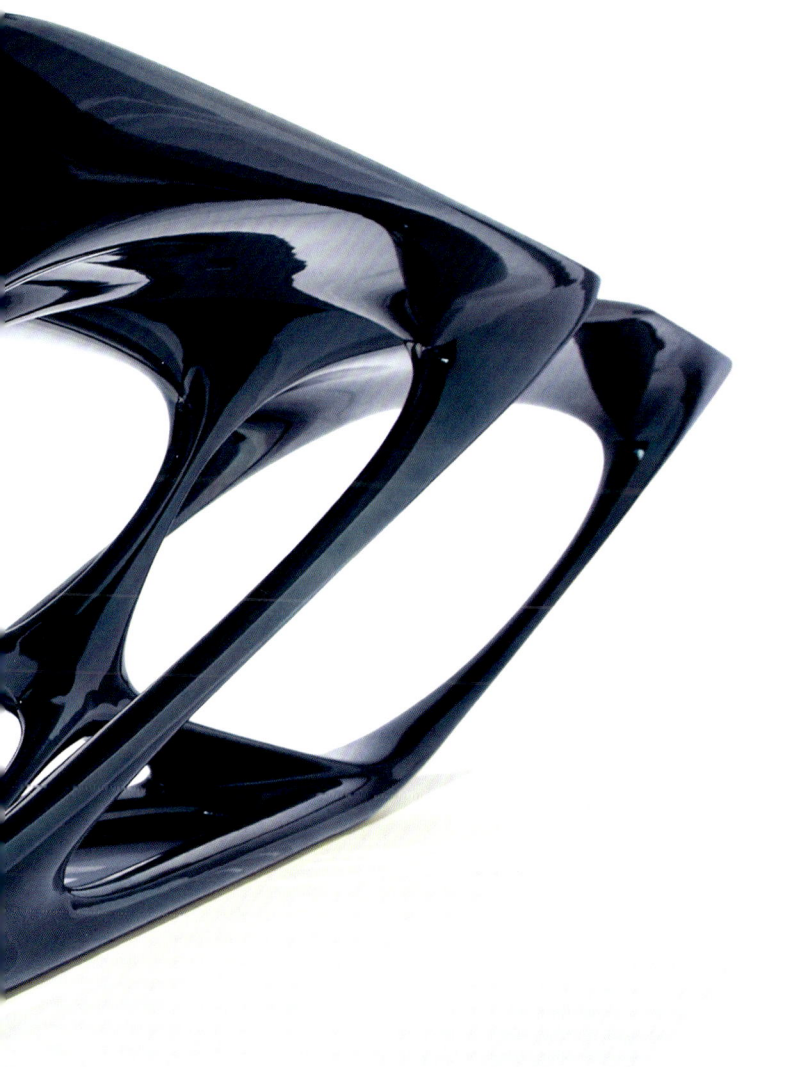

ZAHA HADID
Form in Motion

KATHRYN BLOOM HIESINGER

WITH AN ESSAY BY PATRIK SCHUMACHER

PHILADELPHIA MUSEUM OF ART

in association with

YALE UNIVERSITY PRESS

New Haven and London

Published on the occasion of the exhibition
Zaha Hadid: Form in Motion
Philadelphia Museum of Art
September 17, 2011–March 25, 2012

This exhibition was made possible by Lisa S. Roberts and David W. Seltzer. Additional support was provided by the Graham Foundation for Advanced Studies in the Fine Arts and Collab—a group that supports the Museum's modern and contemporary design collection and programs. Transportation of selected exhibition objects was provided courtesy of Zumtobel Lighting, the Museo Alessi, and Julian A. Treger.

The catalogue was funded by Lisa S. Roberts.

Architect: Zaha Hadid Architects
Design: Zaha Hadid and Patrik Schumacher

Project Director: Woody K.T. Yao
Exhibition Design Team: Jimena Araiza, Filipa Gomes
Exhibition Coordinators: Manon Janssens, Maha Kutay
Press and Communications Coordinators: Roger Howie, Davide Giordano

Pages 2–3: Detail of *Mesa* Table (cat. 4). Courtesy Vitra GmbH. Photograph by Eduardo Perez
Page 6: Design for *Zaha Hadid: Form in Motion*. Courtesy Zaha Hadid Architects
Pages 8–9, 54: Installation views of *Zaha Hadid: Form in Motion* at the Philadelphia Museum of Art. Photographs by Paul Warchol Photography, Inc.
Pages 14–15: Installation view of *Zaha Hadid: Form in Motion* at the Philadelphia Museum of Art. Photograph by Jason Wierzbicki
Pages 24–25: Detail of *Kloris* Seating Elements (cat. 7). Courtesy Zaha Hadid Architects

Philadelphia Museum of Art Bulletin, n.s., no. 4
The *Bulletin* is an occasional publication of the Philadelphia Museum of Art.

Produced by the Publishing Department
Philadelphia Museum of Art
Sherry Babbitt, The William T. Ranney Director of Publishing
2525 Pennsylvania Avenue
Philadelphia, PA 19130 USA
www.philamuseum.org

Published by the Philadelphia Museum of Art
in association with
Yale University Press
P.O. Box 209040
302 Temple Street
New Haven, CT 06520-9040 USA
www.yalebooks.com/art

Edited by David Updike and Sarah Noreika
Production by Richard Bonk
Jacket/cover designed by Zaha Hadid Architects
Text designed by Lisa Benn Costigan
Printed and bound in Canada by Transcontinental Litho Acme, Montreal

Text and compilation © 2011 Philadelphia Museum of Art

"Design is Communication" by Patrik Schumacher © 2011 by the author

Works by Zaha Hadid © Zaha Hadid Architects

All rights reserved. No part of this publication may be reproduced or transmitted in any form or by any means, electronic or mechanical, including photocopying, recording, or any other information storage or retrieval system, without permission in writing from the publisher.

Lenders to the Exhibition

Alessi S.p.A., Crusinallo, Italy
B&B Italia, Novedrate, Italy
Francine and Stuart Gerstein
David Gill Galleries, London
Zaha Hadid Architects, London
Lacoste Footwear, New York
Melissa Shoes, New York
Sawaya & Moroni, Milan
Kenny Schachter / Rove Projects LLP, London
Swarovski North America Limited, Cranston, RI
Valli & Valli USA, New York
Vitra Design Museum, Weil am Rhein, Germany
Private collection

Photography Credits:
B&B Italia: cat. 6 (photograph by Fabrizio Bergamo). Richard Bryant / arcaidimages.com: figs. 2, 3. David Gill Galleries: cat. 5 (photograph by Michael Molloy). David Grandorge: cat. 17. Zaha Hadid Architects: pages 6, 24–25; cats. 11, 12; figs. 5–7, 8 (photograph by Hufton + Crow), 9–11. Luke Hayes: page 59. Lacoste S.A.: cat. 18. Victoria Nightingale: cat. 19 (gold). ORCH: cat. 3. Sawaya & Moroni: cats. 1, 9 (photograph by Ruy Tuixera). Barbara Sorg: cat. 4. Swarovski North America Limited: cat. 15. Kelly Turso: cats. 19 (silver), 20. Vitra GmbH: page 2 (photograph by Eduardo Perez). Paul Warchol Photography, Inc.: pages 8–9, 54; cat. 7; fig. 4. Jason Wierzbicki: pages 14–15; cats. 8, 10, 13, 14, 16. Zumtobel Lighting GmbH: cat. 2

Library of Congress Cataloging-in-Publication Data

Hiesinger, Kathryn B., 1943–
Zaha Hadid : form in motion / Kathryn Bloom Hiesinger ; with an essay by Patrik Schumacher.
    p. cm.
Published on the occasion of an exhibition held at the Philadelphia Museum of Art, Sept. 17, 2011–March 25, 2012.
ISBN 978-0-87633-232-0 (PMA) — ISBN 978-0-300-17982-8 (Yale UP)
1. Hadid, Zaha—Exhibitions. I. Hadid, Zaha. II. Schumacher, Patrik, 1961– III. Philadelphia Museum of Art. IV. Title. V. Title: Form in motion.
NA1469.H33A4 2011
720.92—dc23   2011033817

Foreword 6
TIMOTHY RUB

Design is Communication 10
PATRIK SCHUMACHER

Zaha Hadid: Form in Motion 16
KATHRYN BLOOM HIESINGER

Catalogue 25
KATHRYN BLOOM HIESINGER

Exhibition Design 55
ZAHA HADID ARCHITECTS

Checklist of the Exhibition 56

Zaha Hadid 58
KATHRYN HIGGINS

Glossary 60
KATHRYN HIGGINS

Foreword

As Collab, the group of like-minded individuals who have long supported the development of the Philadelphia Museum of Art's modern and contemporary design collection, celebrates its fortieth anniversary, we are delighted to mark this occasion with a special series of exhibitions and programs. Among the most ambitious of these is *Zaha Hadid: Form in Motion*. That is perhaps as it should be, because Hadid is an architect (and designer: she makes no strong distinction between these two different but complementary fields) of immense ambition. So it has been since she emerged on the international scene nearly thirty years ago with a dynamic and breathtakingly beautiful competition design for a new entertainment complex on Victoria Peak in Hong Kong.

During the past decade, that ambition has been realized in an increasingly impressive series of built works, from transportation centers and office towers to museums and performance halls. Viewed as a whole, these reveal both the maturation of Hadid's distinctive vision of a new architecture dynamically engaged with the context—in the broadest sense of this term—in which it will take its place and a restless (and wholly admirable) desire to innovate.

As this exhibition underscores, Hadid's design practice is not limited to architecture. Working in close collaboration with manufacturers and materials engineers, she has also produced a broad range of functional objects such as furniture, lighting, jewelry, and even footwear. While this predilection does not distinguish her from many of her contemporaries, what does is the close—one could even say integral—relationship she posits between the design of these objects and the architectural setting. This is a longstanding architectural dream, but one to which she has given new life and, more importantly, new meaning.

Thus, visitors to the exhibition will see not only examples of furniture and decorative works of art that Hadid has created in recent years, but also the environment she has designed for their display. It will, I am sure, be a transformative experience for many and help them understand why the members of Collab have decided to present Zaha Hadid with their design award for excellence this year.

We owe our deepest thanks for the success of this project to Zaha Hadid and the commitment she made to work with us; to her design partner Patrik Schumacher for contributing his thoughtful essay to this catalogue; to Project Director Woody K.T. Yao for working so closely with us on the development of the installation design; and to his colleagues at Zaha Hadid Architects—Exhibition Design Team Jimena Araiza and Filipa Gomes, Exhibition Coordinators Manon Janssens and Maha Kutay, and Press and Communications Coordinators Roger Howie and Davide Giordano—for spending countless hours helping to keep our work on time and within budget. We would also like to thank the lenders to this exhibition who so graciously parted with their objects, some contributing to the costs of shipping and restoration. Among the many staff members of the Philadelphia Museum of Art who made significant contributions, several deserve special mention: Kathryn Bloom Hiesinger, our Curator of Decorative Arts after 1700 and the principal organizer of this exhibition, who selected the objects on the checklist in consultation with Zaha Hadid and her staff and authored this catalogue; Jack Schlechter, our Installations Designer, and Jeffrey Sitton, our Installations Design Assistant, who with characteristic thoroughness attended to every detail of the design and installation; Suzanne Wells, our Director of Exhibition Planning, and especially Eliza deForest Johnson, our Assistant Director of Exhibition Planning, without whose patience and resolve this project would not have been a success.

Lastly, and most importantly, I would like to extend our heartfelt appreciation to the several funders of this project, especially Lisa S. Roberts and David W. Seltzer, who have been wonderful supporters of our work and extraordinary advocates for design, and to the members of Collab. We are grateful for their generosity and the collaborative spirit they have brought to their relationship with the Philadelphia Museum of Art. May it last another four decades!

Timothy Rub
The George D. Widener Director and Chief Executive Officer

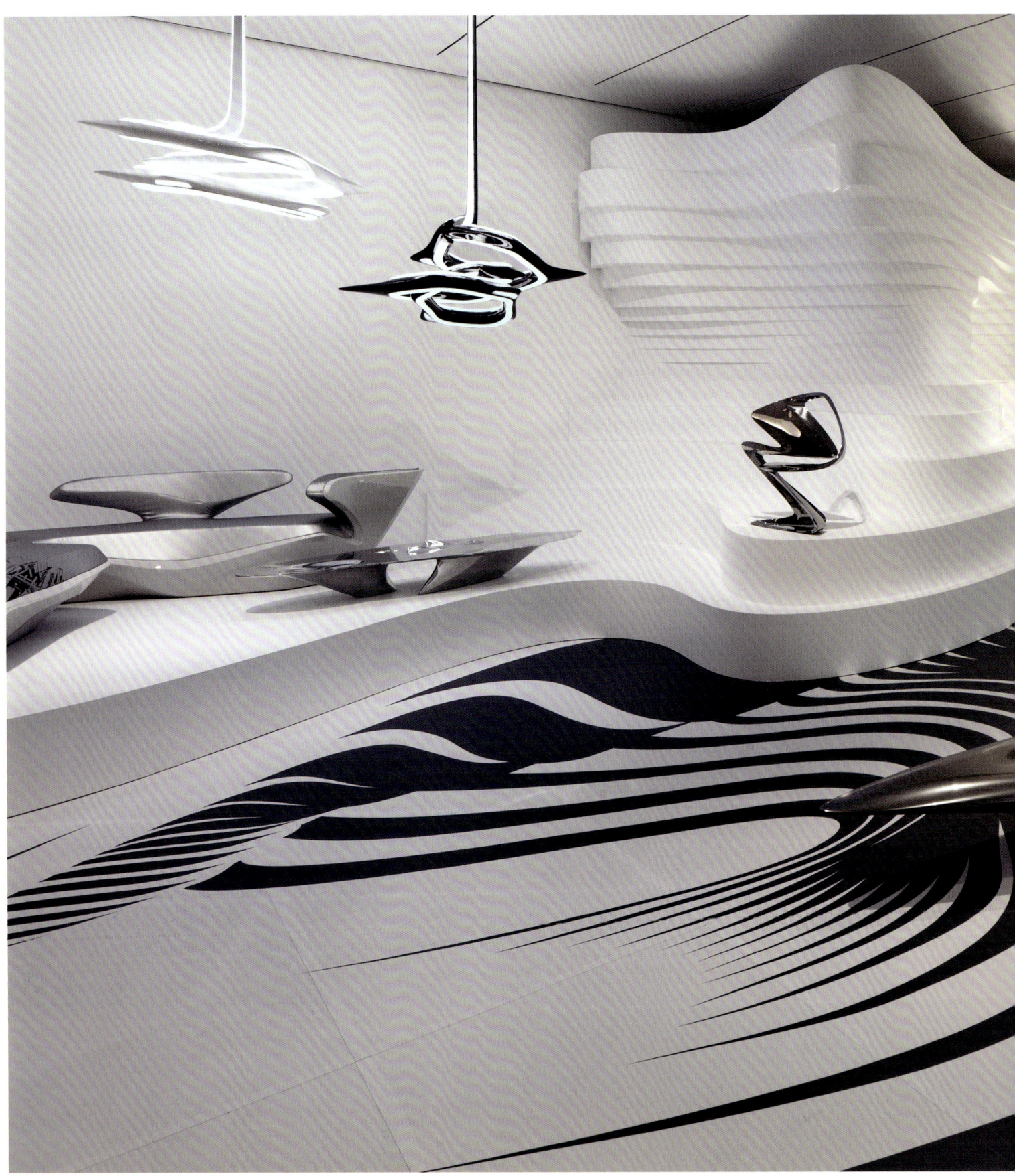

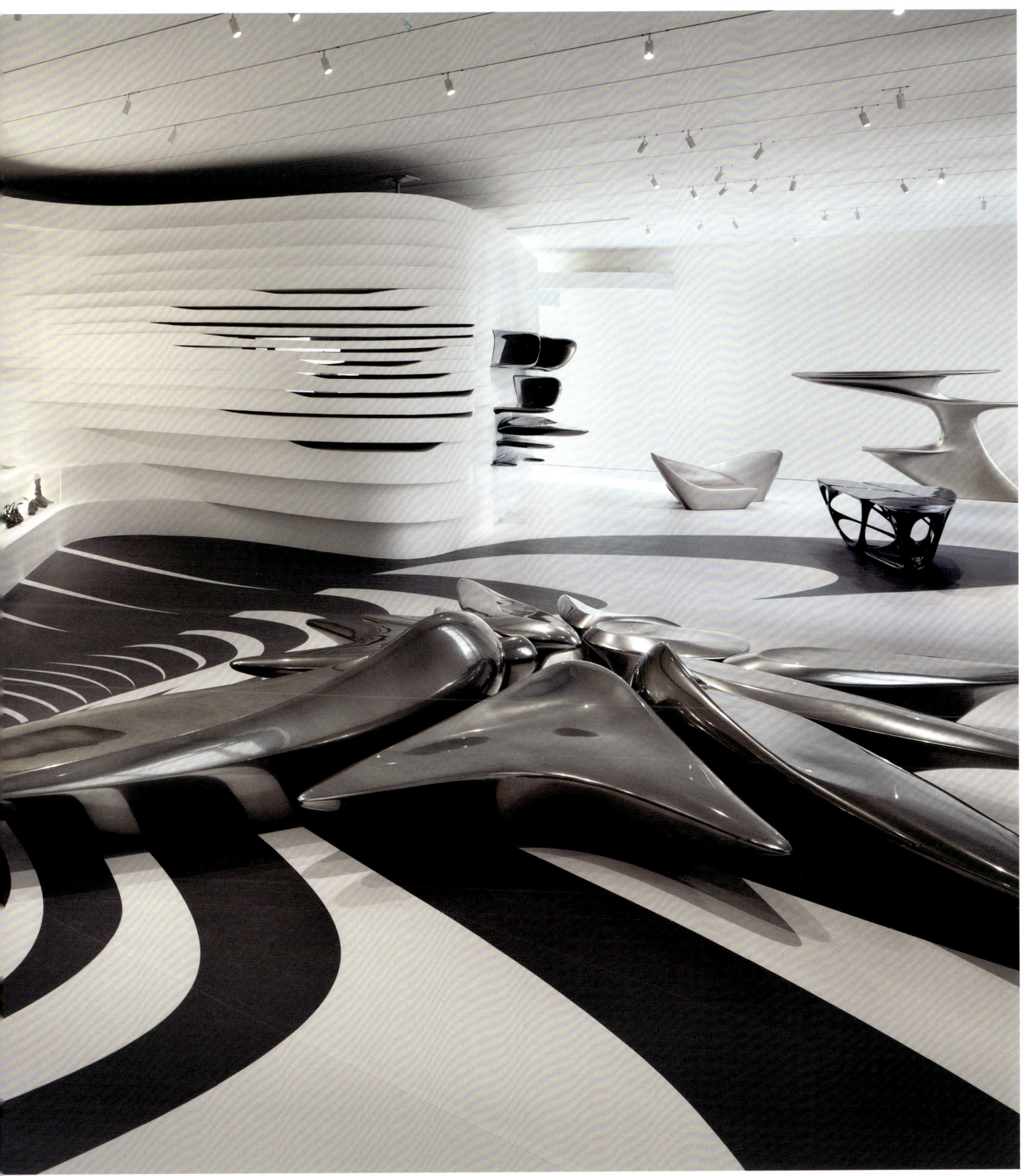

Design is Communication
PATRIK SCHUMACHER

What is design? What are its sui generis discourse and core competency? These questions can be best answered via demarcation from neighboring discourses/competencies such as engineering and art. What is the difference between design and engineering? Engineering is concerned with an object's physical/technical functioning and fabrication, design with its social/communicative functioning. What is the difference between design and art? While design is concerned with the framing of real-life social interactions, the art object communicates outside of everyday life, as reflection, provocation, critique, or even disruption. It confronts the world with the specter of other possibilities. However, these other possibilities cannot be approached via art. They can only be approached via avant-garde design.

While I distinguish design—perhaps with unfamiliar sharpness—from both art and engineering, I draw all the design disciplines together into a single discourse and competency. Urbanism, architecture, and interior design, as well as furniture, fashion, graphic, and product design, together constitute one of the great autopoietic function systems of society. This function system of design is a global discourse—world architecture/design—which claims universal and exclusive competency for the global built environment as well as for the totality of the world's designed artifacts—as long as these built environments and artifacts operate as frames or interfaces of social communication. What all the design disciplines and their products share is their societal function: the *framing* of communicative interaction. With respect to architecture this insight takes the form of an explicit thesis in my book *The Autopoiesis of Architecture*: "Every society needs to utilize articulated spatial relations to frame, order, and stabilize social communication. The autopoietic system of architecture within modern functionally differentiated society has taken up this societal function: to *frame* social communication."[1]

The societal function of the other design disciplines—in particular, product and fashion design—can be defined in terms that are precisely parallel to the above definition of architecture's societal function. The framing of communicative interaction is the societal function of both architecture and design. In fact, the spatial frames of architecture collaborate with the system of designed artifacts in the framing of social communication. Architecture distinguishes, separates, and gathers the participants for specific communications. The interior/furniture configures the participants into pertinent constellations, allocating roles and helping to define specific situations. The participants also dress up for specific occasions. All social interaction is framed by artificial spaces, artifacts, and adornments. We rarely communicate naked in the wilderness. In order to grasp the ordering capacity of architecture (and design and society's dependency upon it), imagine that the ten million people who live and work in a metropolis like London are stranded on a vast, undifferentiated plane, stripped of their clothes and their designed and built environment. Nobody would even know who he or she was anymore, let alone how, with whom, and where to interact. Design sets the scene and prepares the appropriate setting or stage for communicative interaction. Communication can begin only once the participants have been gathered, configured, and enveloped within an appropriate aesthetic atmosphere. Specific social institutions depend on specifically designed frames. A culture can be identified with its system of institutions, which in turn depends upon a system of designed frames. Frames are priming communications, premises that define, guide, and encourage all further communications that unfold within them.[2] Architectural settings are thus to be designed as framing communications, as permanent broadcasts that function as constraining/enabling premises for all further communications that are to be expected within the respective space. Architectural settings are communications that help to define and structure social institutions.[3] Spatial and artifactual frames also allow participants to find and anticipate communicative situations that might be expected with respect to specific settings. Thus the built environment and the world of artifacts constitute an information-rich communicative medium—indeed, a semiotic system. Every talented designer navigates this system intuitively. However, as society and its institutional complexity increase it might become necessary to support the designer's semiological competency by means of theoretical and methodological reflection.[4]

The sociological insight that underlies the identification of design's societal function can be cast into the thesis that no society can be built up without articulated spatial frames, artifacts, and adornments. Even the most basic and precarious human societies ever observed—the Australian tribes, for example—exist and stabilize themselves via pre-architectural and artifactual frames.[5] The built environment—filled with an ever-increasing multitude of artifacts—provides a new material substrate for long-term (cross-generational) social "memory," a necessary foundation for the evolution of social order. Just as biological evolution depends on DNA as the material substrate of its stable, slowly evolving reproduction, sociocultural evolution depends on the built environment as the stable, material substrate of its evolving reproduction. This is the crucial point of bifurcation that engenders the sociocultural evolution of humankind as a new, sui generis type of evolution. Only via this new evolutionary substrate can a new, more complex, artificial order be built up that effectively allows the human species to escape the animal kingdom. The evolution of society goes hand in hand with the evolution of its habitat understood as ordering frame. The spatial order of the human habitat is both an immediate physical ordering apparatus that separates and connects social actors and their activities *and* a mnemotechnic substrate for the inscription of an external "social memory." The social process needs the built environment and the world of artifacts as a plane of inscription where it can leave traces that then serve to build up and stabilize social structures, which in turn allow the elaboration of more complex social processes. These "inscriptions" might at first be an unintended side effect of the various activities. Given spatial arrangements are functionally adapted and elaborated, and then further marked and underlined by ornaments that make them more conspicuous. The result is the gradual build-up of a spatio-morphological system of signification. Thus emerges a semantically charged built environment that provides a differentiated system of settings that help social actors to orient themselves with respect to the different communicative situations that constitute the social life process of the community. The system of social settings as a system of distinctions and relations uses both the positional identification of places (spatial position) and the morphological identification of places (ornamental marking) as props[6] for the social communication process. Indications for this formative nexus between social and spatial structure abound within social anthropology, attesting to the crucial importance of stable spatio-morphological settings for the initial emergence and stabilization of all societies. In the analysis of the social structure of primitive societies, the drawing of the village plan (together with the taxonomy of its tools, clothes, and adornments) often serves as the most succinct summary and point of reference of social order.[7]

Appropriately designed places regulate social communication by helping to define the situation, reminding the actors who they are and ordering them into their appropriate relative positions.

Human society, from its very beginnings, evolved together with a built environment and the world of artifacts. This co-evolution is a universal feature of all human history. The modern constellation whereby the built environment is steered by architecture as a discursively autonomous (autopoietic) function system that co-evolves with several other such function systems—for example, those of science, law, economics, politics, and art—constitutes only the latest mode of this universal feature of human history. As traditional society evolves into modern, functionally differentiated society, the built environment develops from a state of vernacular tradition to one in which it is advanced by the specialized function system of architecture/design. However, the crucial, primordial substrate of sociocultural evolution—the capacity of spatial and artifactual frames to order social communication on ever-increasing levels of complexity—remains vital. It has been taken on by architecture and the design disciplines as their unique responsibility, societal function, and exclusive domain of competency.

This implies a continuous upgrading of architecture/design's capacity to order (organize and articulate) social relations and institutions. Architecture/design progresses via the evolution of styles as the indispensible design research programs of the design disciplines. The great epochal styles—the Gothic, the Renaissance, Baroque, Rococo, Neo-Classicism, Historicism, and Modernism—always encompassed all the design disciplines. In fact, these disciplines were only differentiated during the twentieth century. Parametricism is the most credible candidate to become the new, unified, epochal style for the twenty-first century. Its reach is already global, and its scope is universal, including urbanism, architecture, and interior design, as well as furniture and product design. During the last thirty years we have radically transformed into what one might call a post-fordist network society.[8] The attendant crisis of Modernism engendered a period of radical critique, experimentation, and theoretical confusion. Only recently, in the new millennium, has a new avant-garde movement gathered sufficient strength, coherence, and confidence to establish a global paradigm to succeed Modernism. The societal function of urban and architectural design is the innovative ordering and framing of communication.

Parametricism articulates post-fordist network society by increasing the complexity and intensity of spatial and artifactual communication. Parametricism implies that all elements of architecture and object design have become parametrically malleable, which in turn implies their capacity for adaptive affiliation and a general intensification of relations and communications. Post-fordist network society is characterized by an increased diversity and complexity of communication scenarios. It is the latest/current stage of modern, functionally differentiated society. To remain productive within this society requires a new level of communicative intensity from every individual. Everybody's path must be continuously coordinated and updated within a complex network. The pertinent architectural expression of this is the *field of simultaneity*—in other words, urban spaces in which a rich variety of communicative offerings are presented simultaneously. The visual field is layered in all directions: in front, above, below. This rich manifold is ordered according to gradients and laws of correlation so that hidden layers can be inferred from visible ones. Navigation and orientation are key, as is the nuanced atmospheric priming of social interaction. This poses three key aspects of architecture's task—*organization*, *articulation*, and *signification*, which together constitute architecture's core competency. This leads us from modern space to parametric fields filled with swarms of differentiated and affiliated objects.

Patrik Schumacher is partner at Zaha Hadid Architects (ZHA) and founding director of the Design Research Lab (AADRL) at the Architectural Association School of Architecture in London. He joined ZHA in 1988. Schumacher studied philosophy and architecture in Bonn, London, and Stuttgart, where he received his diploma in architecture in 1990. In 1996 he founded the AADRL with Brett Steele, and continues to serve as one of its co-directors. In 1999 he completed his doctorate at the Institute for Cultural Science, Klagenfurt University, Austria. Since 2004 Schumacher has been a professor at the Institute for Experimental Architecture, Innsbruck University, Austria. Currently he is also a visiting professor at the University of Applied Arts in Vienna.

1. Patrik Schumacher, *The Autopoiesis of Architecture*, vol. 1, *A New Framework for Architecture* (London: John Wiley and Sons, 2011), p. 371. Or to put it more precisely: The societal function of architecture is to continuously adapt and reorder society via contributing to the continuous provision and innovation of the built environment as a framing system of organized and articulated spatial relations.
2. In this respect designed frames are comparable to laws, i.e., the products of the legal system (another of the great function systems of society): laws are also communications that act as guiding premises for many (all) further communications. The same goes for the knowledge provided by the great function system of science.
3. These communications are attributed to the designer's clients rather than the designers themselves, i.e., they are attributed to the occupying institution or hosts of the respectively unfolding communication events.
4. This is what the second volume of *The Autopoiesis of Architecture*, to be published at the end of 2011, will offer. Patrik Schumacher, *The Autopoiesis of Architecture*, vol. 2, *A New Agenda for Architecture* (London: John Wiley and Sons, forthcoming).
5. See Émile Durkheim, *Les formes élémentaires de la vie religieuse: Le système totémique en Australie* (Paris, 1912), published in English as *The Elementary Forms of Religious Life: A Study in Religious Sociology*, trans. Joseph Ward Swain (London: Allen and Unwin, 1915).
6. The term *prop* here means both support structure and equipment for the staging of communication.
7. See, for example, the chapters on social organization in Claude Lévi-Strauss, *Structural Anthropology*, trans. Claire Jacobson and Brooke Grundfest (New York: Basic Books, 1963), pp. 101–63.
8. Post-fordist network society is defined in contrast to Fordist mass society. Fordism is the socioeconomic reproduction system established in the first half of the twentieth century on the basis of the large-scale, assembly-line mass production of a universal consumption standard, including complex consumer durables such as cars, refrigerators, televisions, etc. This reproduction model experienced a crisis during the 1970s, and since then phenomena such as flexible specialization, outsourcing, loosely coupled business networks, alliances, etc., have increased the overall complexity and dynamism of social communication.

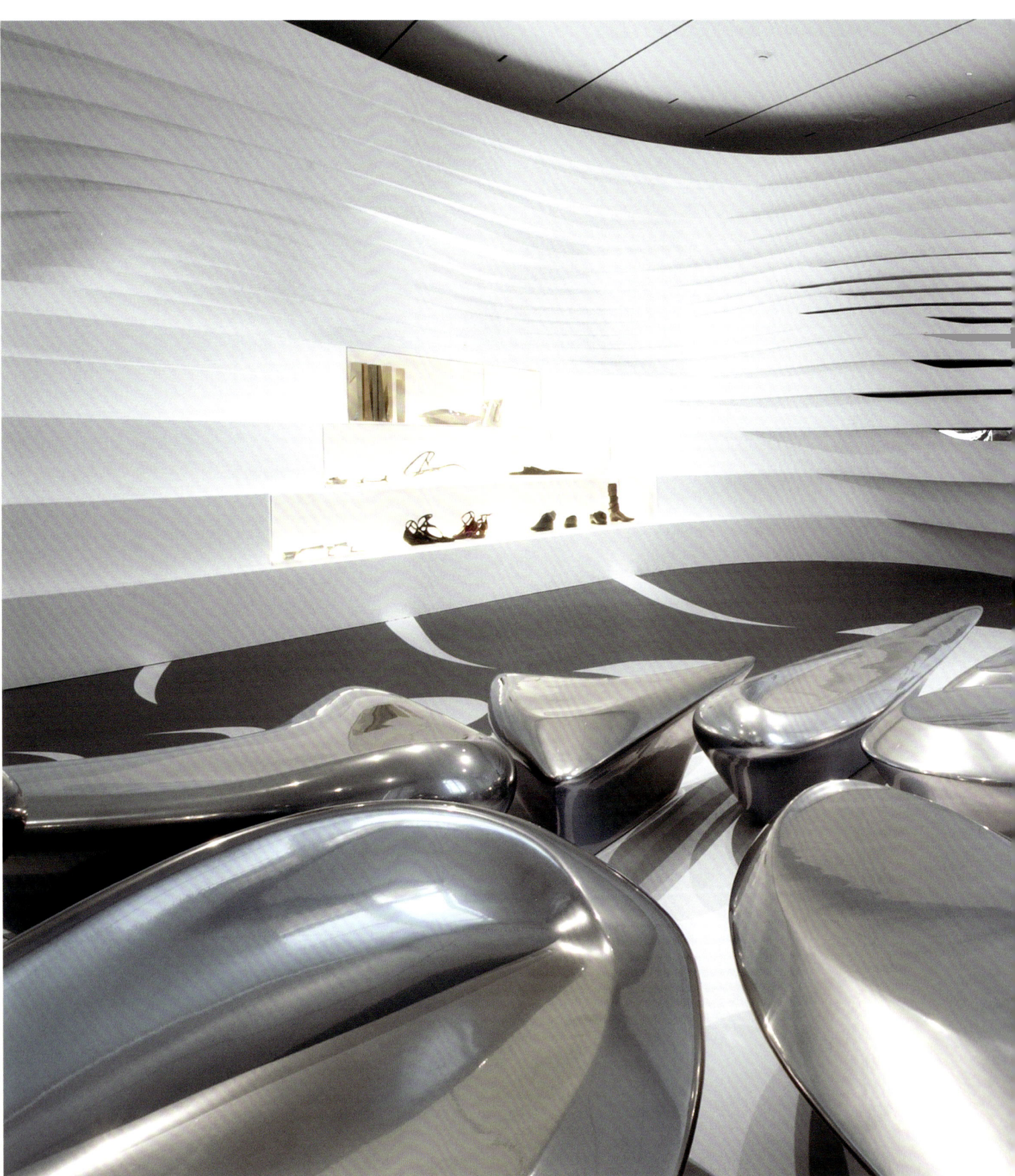

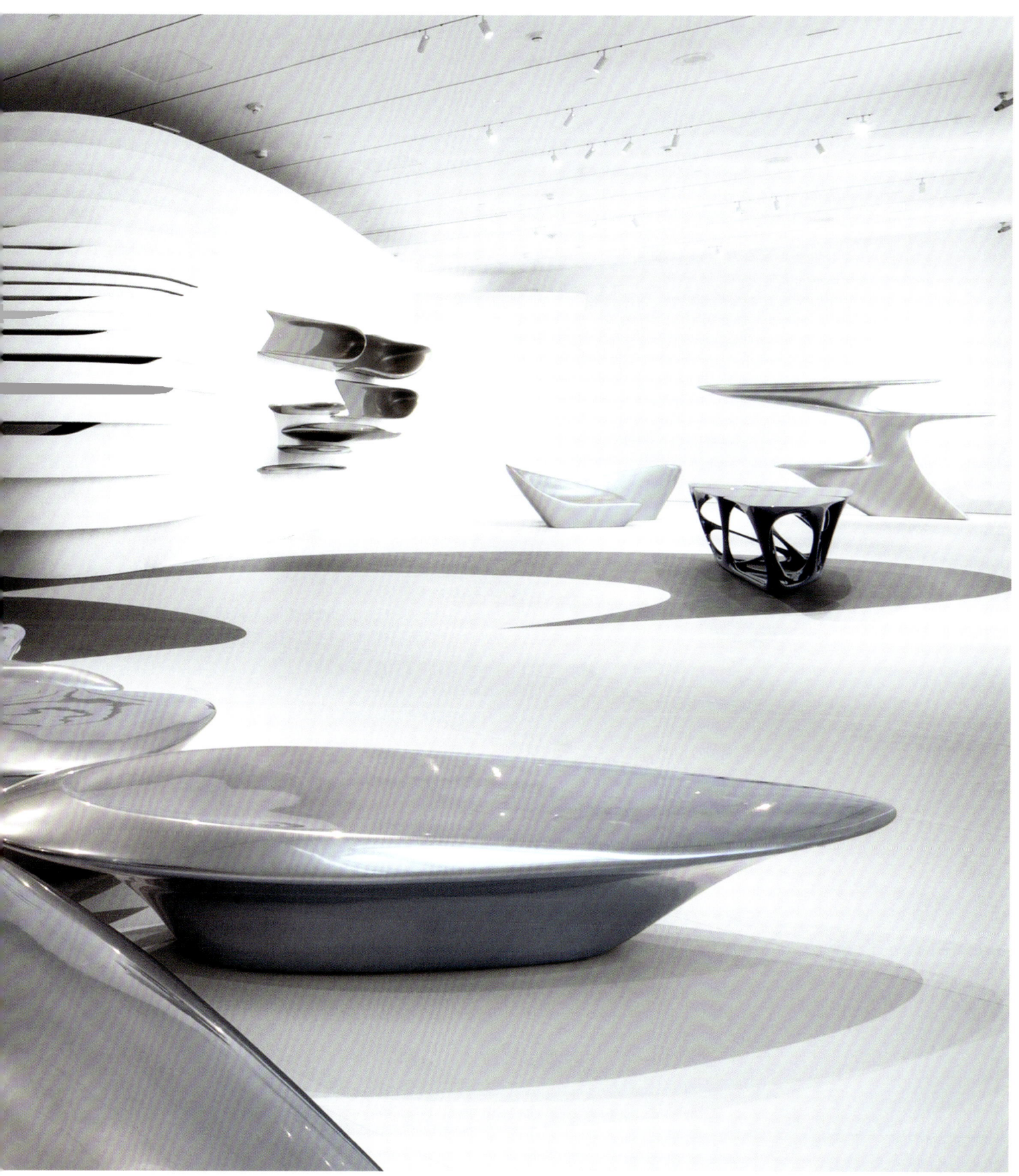

Zaha Hadid: Form in Motion
KATHRYN BLOOM HIESINGER

Zaha Hadid does not differentiate between the practices of architecture, urban planning, and design in her work.[1] Her design language applies to all scales, and she positions herself emphatically as an artist in all three disciplines. Limited in functional requirements and by fabrication complexities, furniture and objects sometimes serve as prototypes for elements of buildings, such as the crisscrossing connectors (themselves derived from architectural experiments) supporting Hadid's *Mesa* table (2007; see cat. 4), which evolved into the branching, interconnecting structural system of the glass curtain wall in the Abu Dhabi Performing Arts Centre (2007; see fig. 6). In equal measure, her furniture and object designs often are informed by architectural research, such as the 2005 *Crevasse* vase series for Alessi (see cat. 19), which developed from Hadid's twin towers design created for the *City of Towers* exhibition at the Eighth International Biennale of Architecture in Venice in 2002. Hadid also thinks across disciplines, as she revealed in a 2004 interview when describing her Phaeno Science Center in Wolfsburg, Germany (2000–2005), as being "like a large table, let's say, with very big legs programmed and made active the whole day and all evening. And then the top of the table, the roof, is where the museum is. The legs are kind of like cones but they, obviously, don't have a point because they have a program. For example, one is a kiosk, one is a bookshop, one is a shop, one is a laboratory, one is the theater."[2]

As a practitioner of interrelated disciplines, Hadid employs her skills in mathematics and painting to inform and synthesize her work. She studied mathematics at the American University in Beirut, Lebanon, before attending architecture school in London; this foundation plays a dominant role in her ability to develop complex geometric shapes with precision and to imagine and realize the advanced engineering her forms require. "I remember wanting to become an architect from a very young age," she recalled, "but I was also very good at math and was always intrigued by the field of modern mathematics and the connection between philosophy, math and physics. This became a short diversion for me."[3] In London, where she studied at the Architectural Association School of Architecture, Hadid developed her own representational technique of drawing and painting to depict the plans, sections, and elevations of buildings. Her colored, abstract studies, which included spatial mapping, projective geometry, and diagrammatic programming, conveyed the expressive energy she wanted her projects to communicate. Hadid's technique, which contrasted sharply with the traditional drawings presented in architectural practice, came to be widely influential, helping to reinvigorate the discipline of architectural drawing. When asked how her unusual style originated, she replied:

> It all started with me drawing to represent a project in a non-conventional way. . . . In time these drawings, projections and paintings became a design tool. . . . We do them at the beginning, in the middle, all the way across. So they are more like very elaborate sketches, it is like sketching and testing out different aspects. . . . Sometimes when you are drawing, you think of another design for another project. . . . It is a very strange way of working but for me it is very exciting.[4]

Inspired as a student by the ideas of early modern Russian artist-theorists, Hadid combined their pictorial devices with her skills in mathematics and fine arts to create a new formal language of architecture and design. Distorted, fragmented, layered, and interpenetrating shapes in non-Euclidean spaces were rendered according to isometric and perspective drawing techniques adapted from the Russian Suprematists, whose interests in technology and in the portrayal of dynamic movement resonated with Hadid. "I am fascinated by the mind of logic and the abstract," she told an interviewer in 2008. "The Russian avant-garde movement of the twenties, the world of Malevich and Kandinsky, brings this together and injects the idea of motion and energy in architecture, giving a feeling of flow and movement in space."[5] In his Suprematist manifesto of 1920, Kazimir Malevich (1878–1935) determined that "form clearly points to the dynamic state of a situation" and called for "the smooth harnessing of form to natural processes."[6] Representing and interrelating forms (and spaces) in motion have been central to Hadid's work since her student days, although her ability to realize these formal dynamics necessarily has depended on advances in digital and material technologies, as demonstrated by the differences between her hand-hammered tea and coffee service for Sawaya & Moroni (1995–96; see cat. 10) and her bowl for the same firm a decade later (2007; see cat. 14), which was realized with digital direct-to-manufacturing technology. Hadid also has explored the representation of what Malevich called "natural processes"; her design vocabulary is conceptually inspired by morphological forms, including botanical (see cat. 7), biological, and geological formations (see cat. 5; fig. 1), as well as organizational and structural systems, the latter tested in a series of building projects from about 1995 to 2000 and realized in her *Z Scape* system of furniture (see cat. 1).

Residential designs were among Hadid's earliest projects after she opened her own office in London. She traces her interest in furniture and interior design to her childhood:

> When I was seven I went with my parents to Beirut to see some new furniture that they had ordered for our home. My father, Mohammed Hadid, was a forward-looking man with cosmopolitan interests. . . . I can still remember going to the furniture-maker's studio and seeing our new furniture. The style was angular and

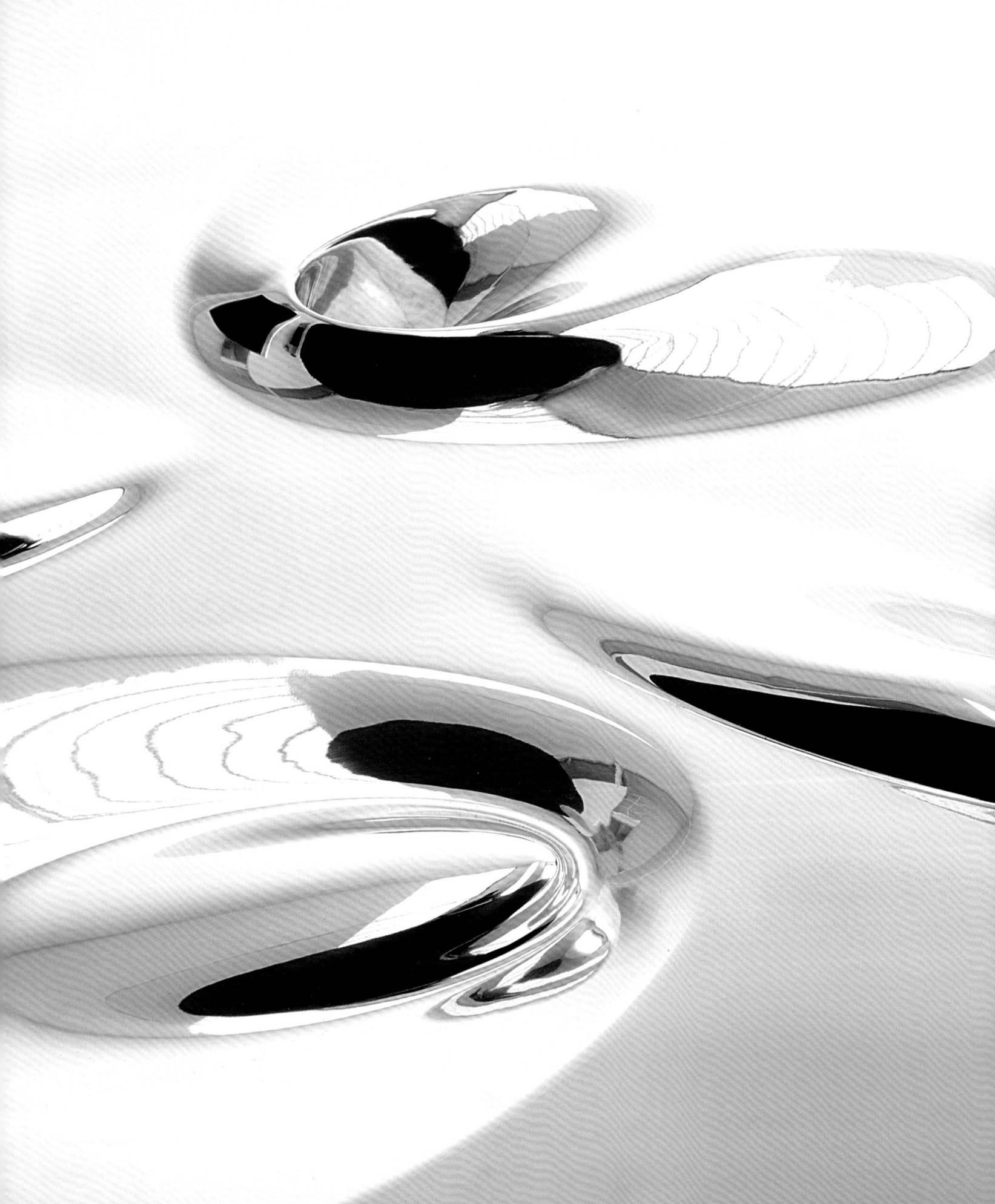

modernist, finished in a chartreuse color, and for my room there was an asymmetric mirror. I was thrilled by the mirror and it started my love of asymmetry. When we got home, I reorganized my room. It went from being a little girl's room to a teenager's. My cousin liked what I had done and asked me to do hers, then my aunt asked me to design her bedroom, and so it started.[7]

Her first realized project was not a building but five pieces of furniture—two tables, two sofas, and a storage unit—designed for timber importer William Bitar's townhouse at 24 Cathcart Road in Kensington, London (1985–86; figs. 2, 3). According to Hadid, the Cathcart Road furniture developed from her idea to create an environment in which furniture pieces act as enclosures and dividers, an architectural concept she has applied consistently, as in her large double-sided *Zephyr* sofa (2010; see cat. 8) and *Moon System* sofa (2007; see cat. 6) and in installations such as her *Ideal House*, designed for the IMM Cologne furniture fair (2007). In a 1987 interview with her former architecture professor Alvin Boyarsky, she described the Cathcart Road furniture as elements in a landscape, "each with its own life. At the same time, they would help to organize the plan."[8] Color was an important factor in these pieces—as it has been throughout her career—though she used it very selectively, relying on a neutral palette against which the stronger colors play:

> The shapes and the materials were very important. They had to be light, as if liberated from certain gravitational forces. . . . When you walk into that space everything is white, but as it opens, color explodes. The same is true of the furniture, which was supposed to be all off-white. As it turns out, one sofa is white with some gray and black (it also has a black backrest) while the other was injected with a single color—yellow. . . . The yellow sofa is not just a sofa; it also acts as a partition or shield. The seat is not only a seat; it could also be a tray.[9]

Constructing the furniture posed challenges for Hadid, particularly engineering the cantilevers so that the sofas appeared to float. She explained: "After making the furniture, I realized that just as I had to invent a new language for drawing and painting, I also had to reinvent certain detailing methods."[10] The fabricators were understandably challenged by Hadid's exceptional designs with their disparate parts, including an oversized, angled sofa (dubbed "woosh") with two separate backrests—each differently shaped and upholstered—cantilevered over a painted steel base; a bronze table base cast as a squiggly, whiplash line with a glass top (the "spermatozoon," or sperm table); and the three-part "wavy-back" sofa (see fig. 3), comprising an undulating backrest fixed to the wall, a fabric-covered bench cantilevered on a wedge-shaped base, and a sculptural wooden nook offering privacy. Composed of seemingly incongruous forms and materials, but visually unified by their exuberant curves and implied movement, the furniture proved to one reviewer that Hadid was "ready to confront the challenges of mass production."[11] In fact, the newly established Italian furniture firm Edra approached Hadid about reproducing the sofas, and introduced the *Woosh*, *Wavy*, and *Projection* sofas (the latter similarly composed of differently shaped and finished parts) at the 1988 Salone Internazionale del Mobile in Milan.[12] This was Hadid's first commercial design commission.

The following year, Hadid created a wildly inventive interior and furnishings for the Monsoon Restaurant in Sapporo, Japan (1989–90; fig. 4). The icy formal dining room, painted in cool grays, was distinguished by sharp, sculptural fragments of glass and metal; the bar, in fiery hot reds, oranges, and yellows, featured an illuminated orange-peel-like spiral curling from the domed ceiling (in implied movement, if not in form or technology, a precursor to Hadid's *Vortexx* chandelier [2005; see cat. 2]), as well as sofas with removable backrests. The idea that furniture (and objects) can be transformed for multiple uses has persisted in her work, such as in the variable elements of the *Dune Formations* (2007; see cat. 3). In 1995, Hadid began her ongoing collaboration with the Italian furniture, accessories, and silverware firm of Sawaya & Moroni with a silver tea and coffee service that is both sculptural and functional (see cat. 10). As uncompromising in its radical innovation as any of Hadid's earlier

Fig. 1. Detail of *Crater* table, 2007 (see cat. 5)

designs, the service is based on a Suprematist strategy of fragmenting and reassembling diagonal forms. The silver was made by hand from two-dimensional, manually drafted specifications, a practice that would soon become obsolete in her office, Zaha Hadid Architects (ZHA), as digital technology advanced during the 1990s and 2000s.

With the arrival of computer-aided design (CAD) and computer-aided manufacturing (CAM), which could produce object-oriented, three-dimensional computer models and feed them directly into a manufacturing system, Hadid could represent and fabricate nonstandard shapes with increasing facility. Although her early designs were erroneously thought to have been influenced by the computer, she in fact has said that she "resisted digitization for a very long time." When she did make the transition, she found that "it wasn't very complicated because the computing almost imitated the way we worked."[13] Although she still paints and draws with pen and ink, the computer is now an integral part of her creative process:

> I have five screens . . . different projects. . . . You work on developing, oh, a table while at the same time you're developing masterplans. It's like you have different information coming from different directions. Like photography. Out of focus . . . then you zoom in. I'll have a sketch—it'll take a few times before it takes. Sometimes a few years. You see, not every idea can be used right then. But nothing is lost. Nothing.[14]

Hadid's personal style began to shift and evolve around "1988 or 1989," she recalls. "My earlier projects were still very planar, but my work began to be about volumes—the position of planes and how they could project into

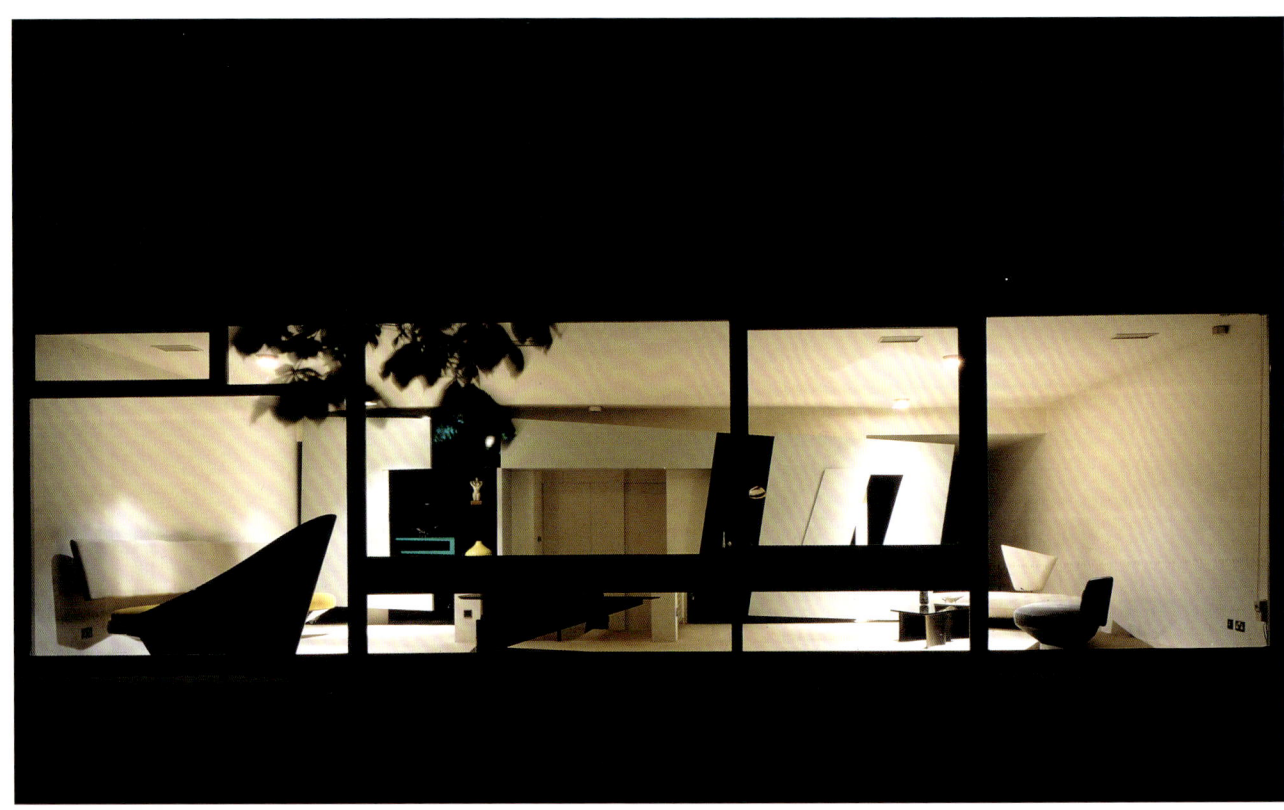

Fig. 2. Exterior view of 24 Cathcart Road, London (1985–86). Courtesy Richard Bryant / arcaidimages.com
Fig. 3. "Wavy-back" sofa, 24 Cathcart Road, London. Courtesy Richard Bryant / arcaidimages.com

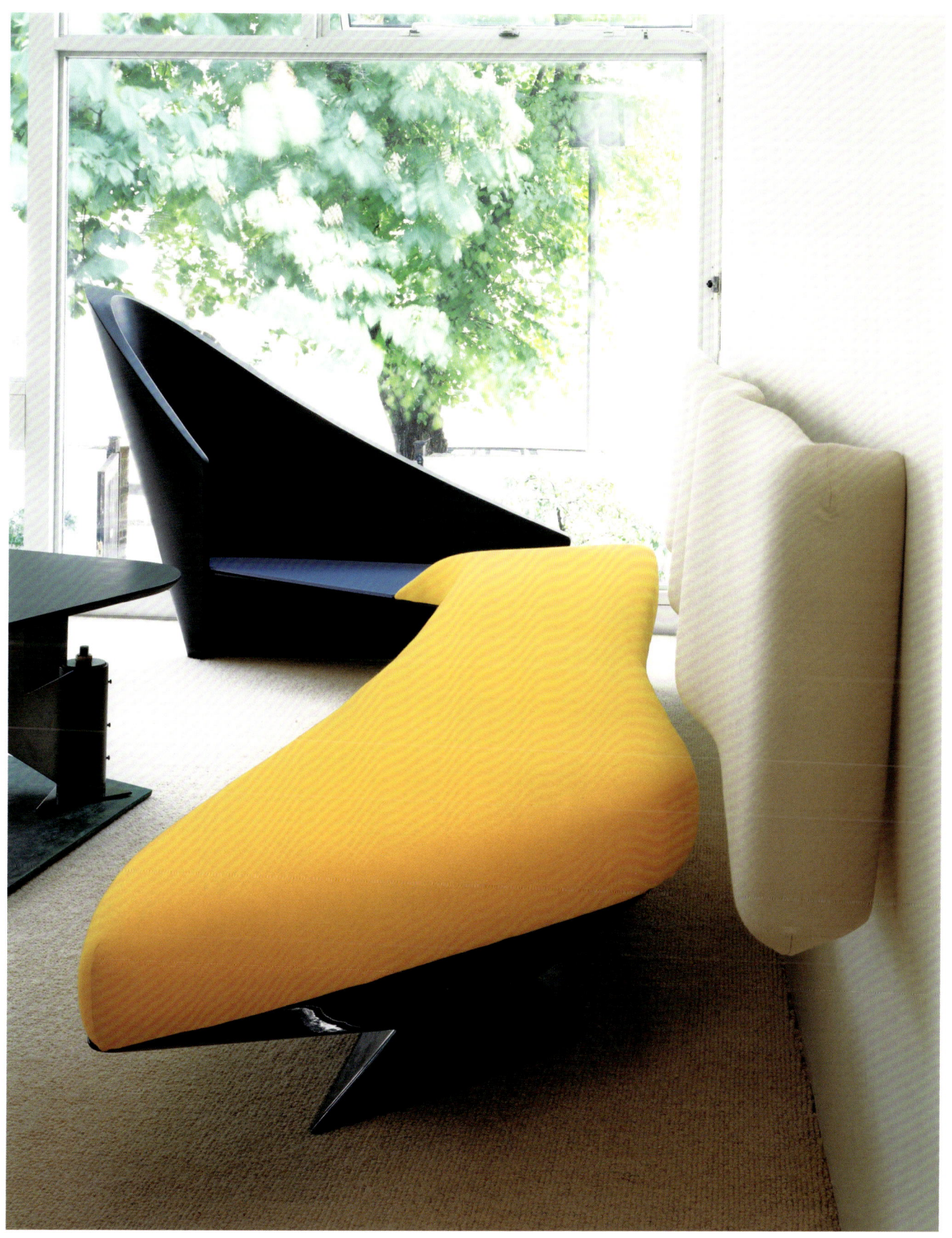

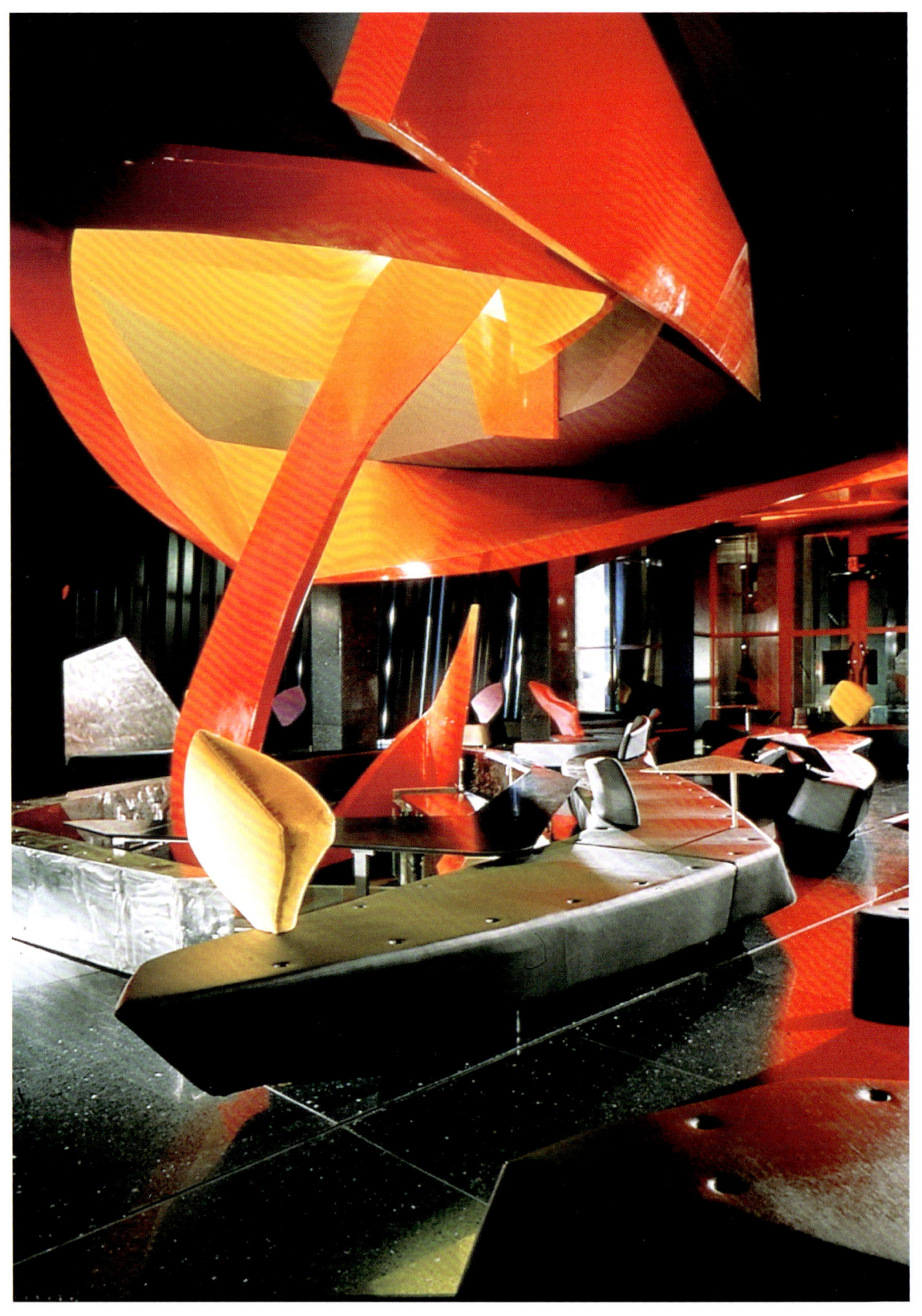

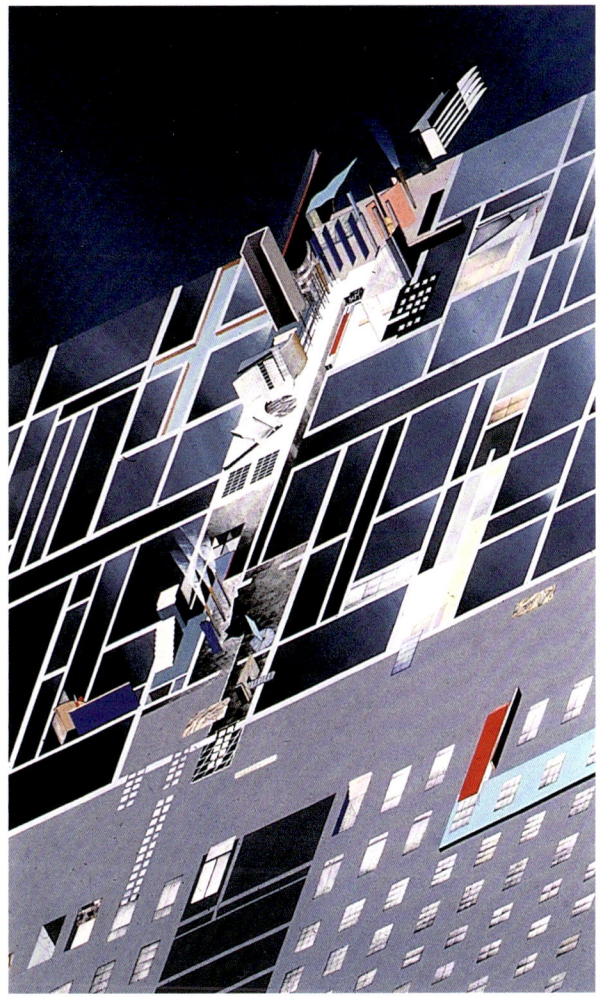

volumes."[15] Especially after 2000, Hadid's early angular forms gradually softened and gave way to a new fluid, curvilinear, formal vocabulary she has applied consistently throughout her work, from an automobile prototype (2005–6; see cat. 11) to resin and crystal jewelry for Swarovski (2009; see cat. 15). Hadid had used curving forms (which she associated with the idea of comfort) in her Cathcart Road furniture as well as in an earlier unrealized proposal for her brother's house at 59 Eaton Place in London (1981–82; fig. 5).

> One of the first times I did a limp curved seat was for my brother. . . . I was always interested in the notion of anticorner seating. Corners don't need to be right angles; they can be much more fluid, like curves. . . . These ideas developed from the language of The Peak [1982–83], and after that our project in Berlin [1986], where we expanded on the whole notion of the curve, creating a very shallow curve, like a boomerang.[16]

The integration of computer software programs such as Maya and RhinoCAD into the office environment from about 2004 has allowed ZHA to render the complex curving surfaces and nonrepeating geometries that appear in Hadid's recent work, including her footwear designs for Melissa (2008; see cat. 17) and Lacoste (2009; see cat. 18). Moreover, differentiating itself from other design firms, ZHA has capitalized on direct-to-production

Fig. 4. Monsoon Restaurant in Sapporo, Japan (1989–90). Photograph © Paul Warchol Photography, Inc.
Fig. 5. Zaha Hadid, *Exploded Axonometric*, painting for 59 Eaton Place, London (1981–82). Courtesy Zaha Hadid Architects, London

technologies, translating designs into finished products that range from table sculptures to a group of seating elements (see cat. 7). As the number of ZHA projects realized continues to grow, the firm has pursued cross-industry fabrication methods that can materialize Hadid's idiosyncratic forms with ease, economy, and speed.

Not only does Hadid incorporate emerging technologies into her design process, her bold imagination continues to push the available material technology forward, as in her door handles for Valli & Valli, which required a specially developed alloy that could be die-cast into a complex shape (2007; see cat. 13), or the folded interior panels in the rooms of the Hotel Puerta America in Madrid (2003–5), where the Valli & Valli door handles were installed, which tested the bending tolerance of their unique thermoformed material. Reaching beyond typical building material manufacturers, ZHA has used yacht and automotive materials such as fiber-reinforced plastic (FRP) in the cladding of her Chanel Mobile Art Pavilion (a traveling exhibition space given by Chanel to the Institut du Monde Arabe, Paris, in 2011), while carbon-fiber-reinforced polymers (CFRP) originally developed for the aerospace industry are intended for use in the working model of Hadid's *Z-Car* (2005–6; see cat. 11). In the end, of course, as in the beginning, Hadid's practice still depends on her ability to create form. "The idea has to be very clear," she has said. "It can't get confused. As long as there is clarity in the idea, you can change other things."[17]

1. I would like to acknowledge with gratitude the assistance of Kathryn Higgins in surveying the literature and for her many other invaluable contributions to this project. I am also indebted to Roger Howie, Thomas Vietzke, Manon Janssens, Jimena Araiza, and Maha Kutay of Zaha Hadid Architects for providing information about their firm's processes and commercial products.
2. Zaha Hadid, interview by Terry Gross, *Fresh Air*, National Public Radio, May 26, 2004, reprinted in Ruth Peltason and Grace Ong-Yan, eds., *Architect: The Work of the Pritzker Prize Laureates in Their Own Words* (New York: Black Dog and Leventhal, 2010), p. 86.
3. "Zaha Hadid," interview by Yoshio Futagawa, in *Studio Talk: Interview with 15 Architects* (Tokyo: A.D.A. Edita, 2002), p. 608.
4. "Entrevista con Zaha Hadid / Interview with Zaha Hadid," Richard Levene and Fernando Márquez Cecilia, in "Zaha M. Hadid," special issue, *El Croquis*, no. 52 (January 1992), pp. 10–11.
5. Zaha Hadid, interview by Vinny Lee, *London Times*, April 19, 2008, reprinted in Peltason and Ong-Yan, *Architect*, p. 90.
6. Kazimir Malevich, "Suprematism: 34 Drawings" (1920), reprinted in Patricia Railing, ed., *Malevich on Suprematism: Six Essays, 1915 to 1926* (Iowa City: University of Iowa Museum of Art, 1999), p. 84.
7. Hadid, interview by Lee, p. 90.
8. "Interview: Alvin Boyarsky Talks with Zaha Hadid," in *Zaha Hadid*, exh. cat. (New York: Solomon R. Guggenheim Museum, 2006), p. 49.
9. Ibid., p. 48.
10. Ibid., pp. 49, 51.
11. Deborah K. Dietsch, "Furniture by Zaha Hadid: AA Bar and Member's Room," *AA Files: Annals of the Architectural Association School of Architecture*, no. 17 (spring 1989), p. 76. See also Deborah K. Dietsch, "A Room of One's Own: Living Room Suite, London," *Architectural Record*, vol. 175, no. 11 (September 1987), pp. 84–88.
12. Karen D. Stein, "The 1988 Salone del Mobile: Making It in Milan," *Architectural Record*, vol. 177 (January 1989), p. 45.
13. Zaha Hadid, "Interview IV—Marathon Interview, from the Serpentine Gallery," by Rem Koolhaas and Hans Ulrich Obrist, London, July 28–29, 2006, in Hans Ulrich Obrist, *Zaha Hadid*, The Conversation Series 8 (Cologne: Buchhandlung Walther König, 2007), p. 89.
14. Zaha Hadid, interview by Jonathan Meades, *Intelligent Life* (summer 2008), http://moreintelligentlife.com/story/zaha-hadid.
15. "Zaha Hadid," interview by Futagawa, p. 618.
16. "Interview: Alvin Boyarsky," p. 49. The Peak was Hadid's proposal for a leisure club in Hong Kong; the Berlin project was a proposal for an office building on Kurfürstendamm.
17. "Zaha Hadid," interview by Futagawa, p. 626.

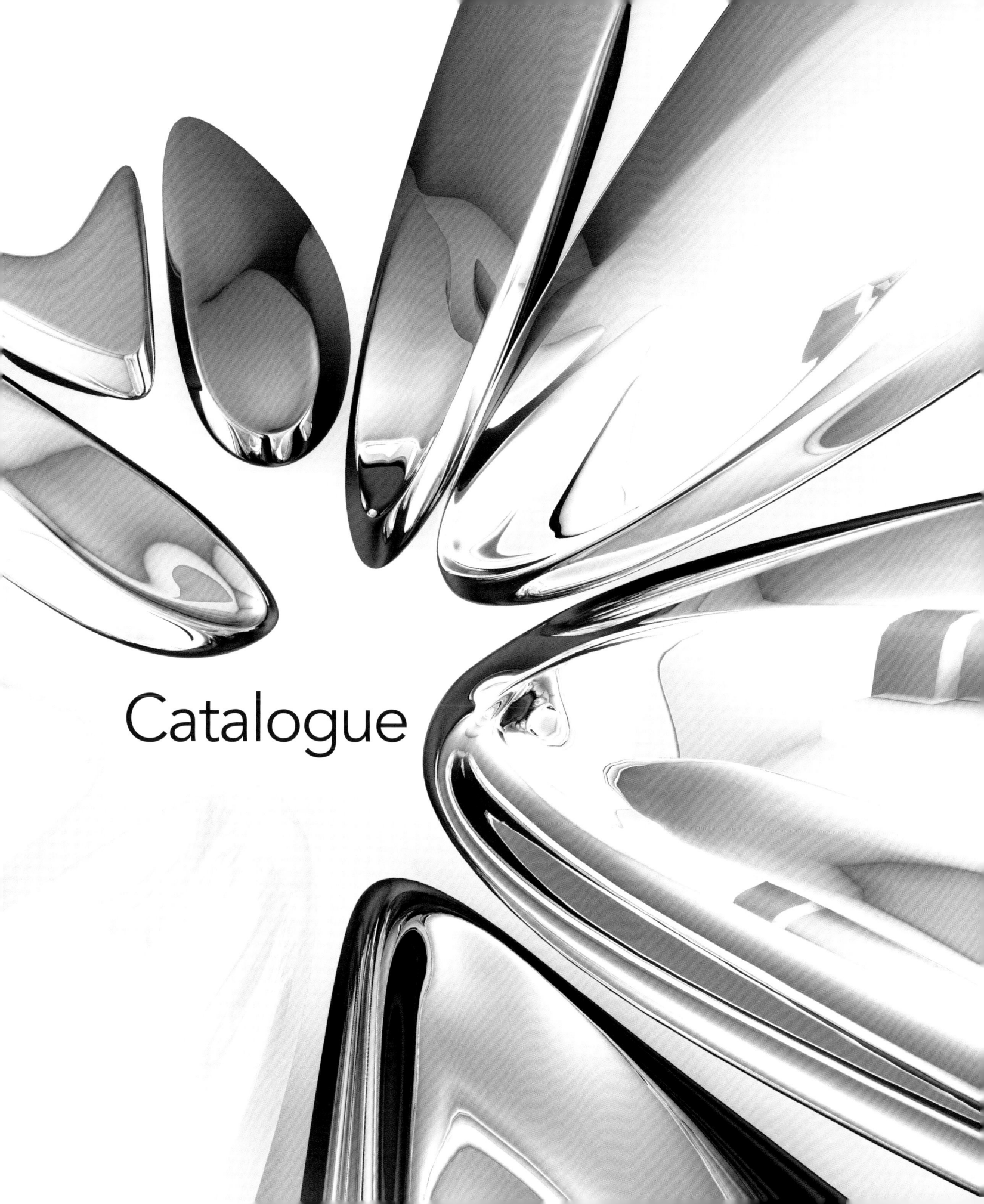

Catalogue

Cat. 1
Z-Play **Seating Elements** | 2002
Made by Sawaya & Moroni
Cold-foamed polyurethane, wool upholstery; W (each piece) 28⅜" (72 cm)
Lent by Sawaya & Moroni

These abstract, irregularly shaped seats are additions to the original *Z-Scape* furniture program of eleven pieces designed by Hadid for Sawaya & Moroni in 2000, when the "morphological" vocabulary she had been exploring throughout her career could first be realized in exact detail with new digital design and manufacturing technologies. Having researched and found inspiration in the morphology of geological forms and stratifications, ZHA was able to transfer Hadid's original drawings directly from the three-dimensional computer model through the CAD/CAM software into the CNC milling machine where the polyurethane foam seats were cut and shaped. Conceived as fragments of a dynamic landscape formation, the seats offer multiple possibilities for use and configuration.

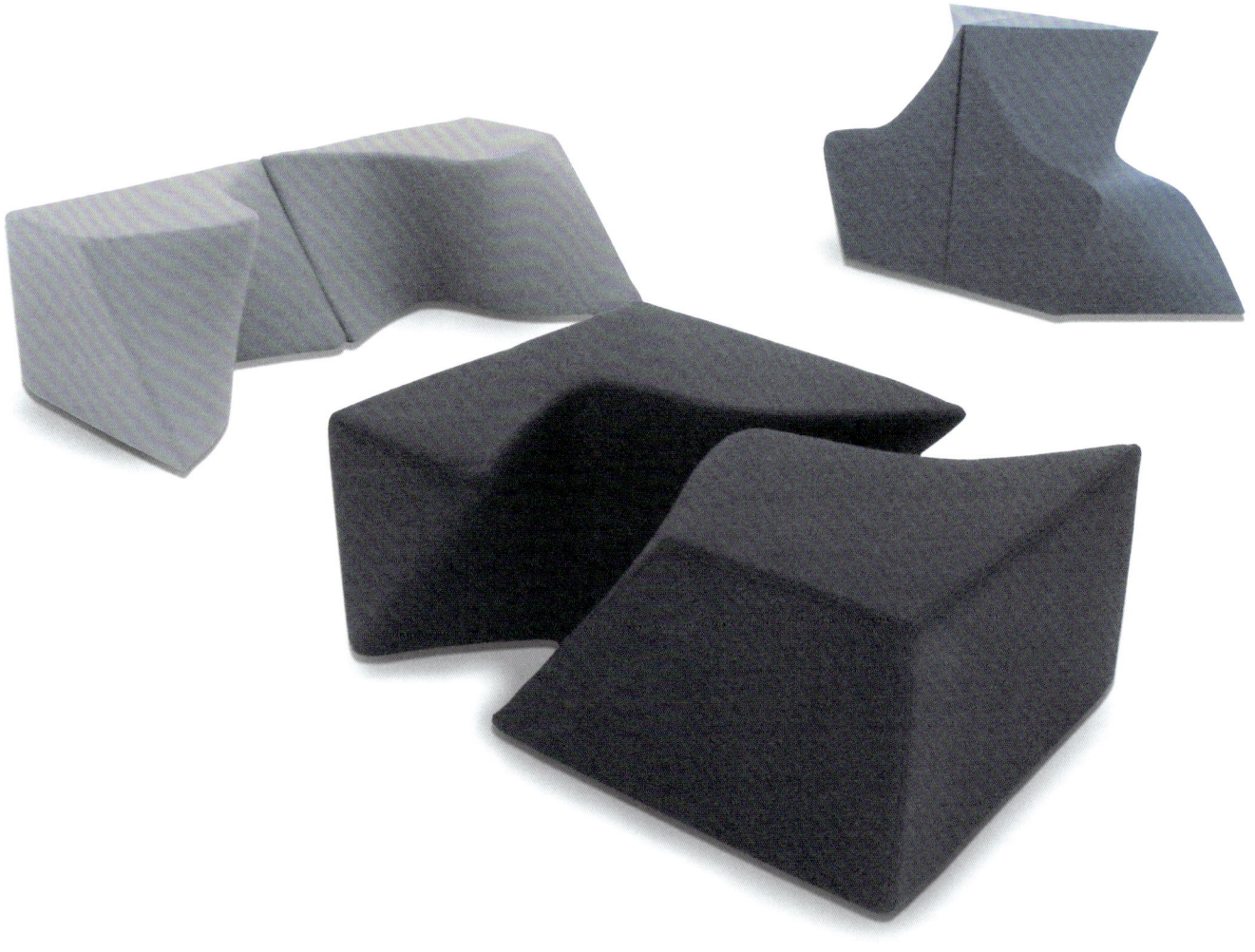

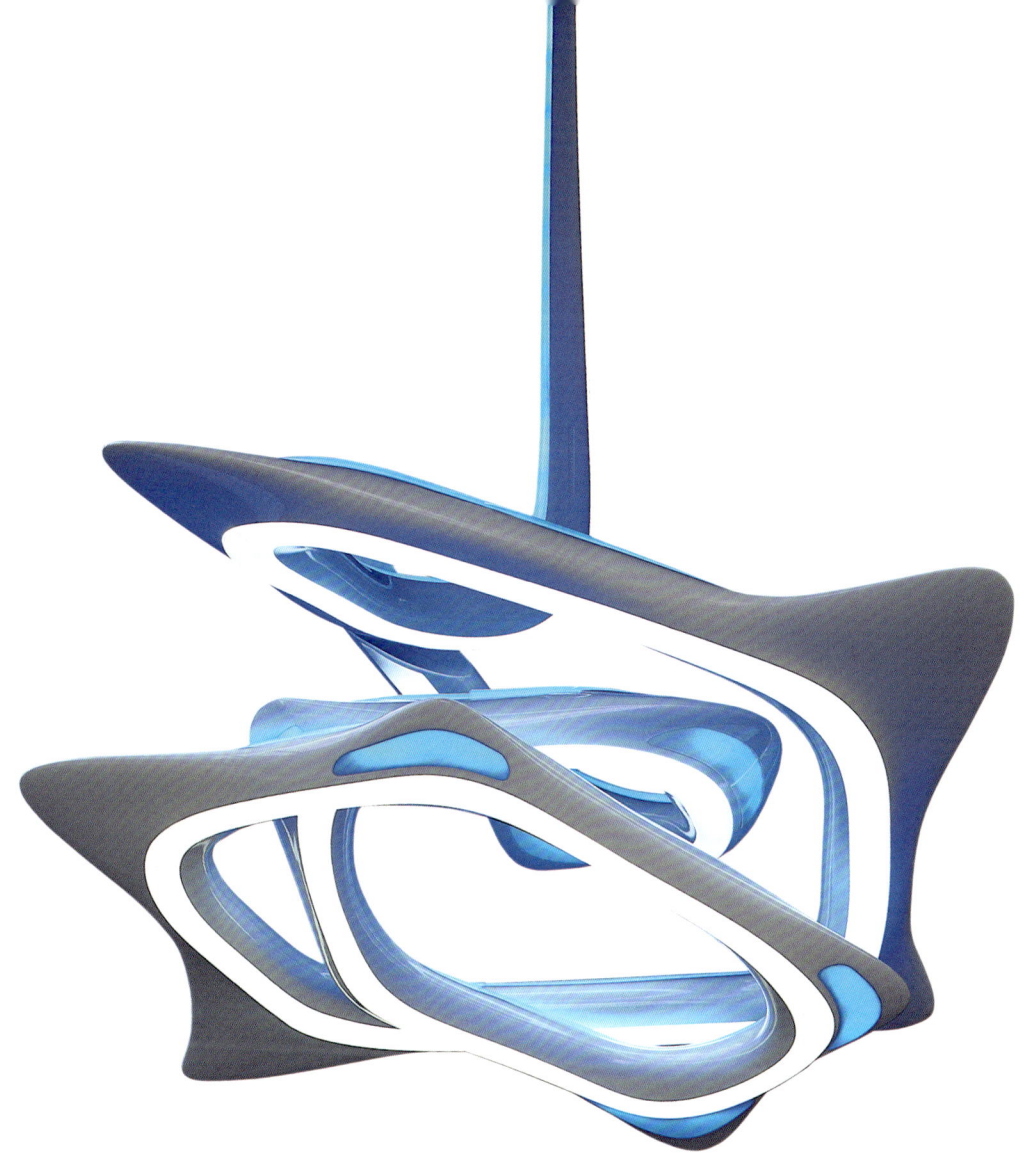

Cat. 2
***Vortexx* Chandelier** | 2005
Made by Zumtobel Lighting GmbH in collaboration with Sawaya & Moroni
Fiberglass, car paint, acrylic, LED; H 60" (152.4 cm)
Private collection

Whirling around a vertical axis, as its name aptly describes, Hadid's *Vortexx* chandelier, made by Zumtobel and produced in collaboration with Sawaya & Moroni, was introduced at Euroluce, the biennial international lighting trade fair in Milan, in April 2005. The following year the chandelier was awarded a prize in the Lights of the Future design competition established by the European Commission to promote energy-efficient residential lighting. Concealed within two spiraling translucent acrylic diffusers cased in fiberglass, colored LED modules are combined with white LEDs that emit light only on the underside. Lower in energy consumption, cooler, smaller, and more durable than incandescent lights, the color-changing LEDs realize Hadid's vision of seamless continuity, so firmly rooted in her recent work. The color of the chandelier changes continuously and almost imperceptibly, flowing through the helical tubes in what appears to be perpetual motion. *Vortexx* is fitted with a programmable management system that allows the user to control the intensity and color of the light.

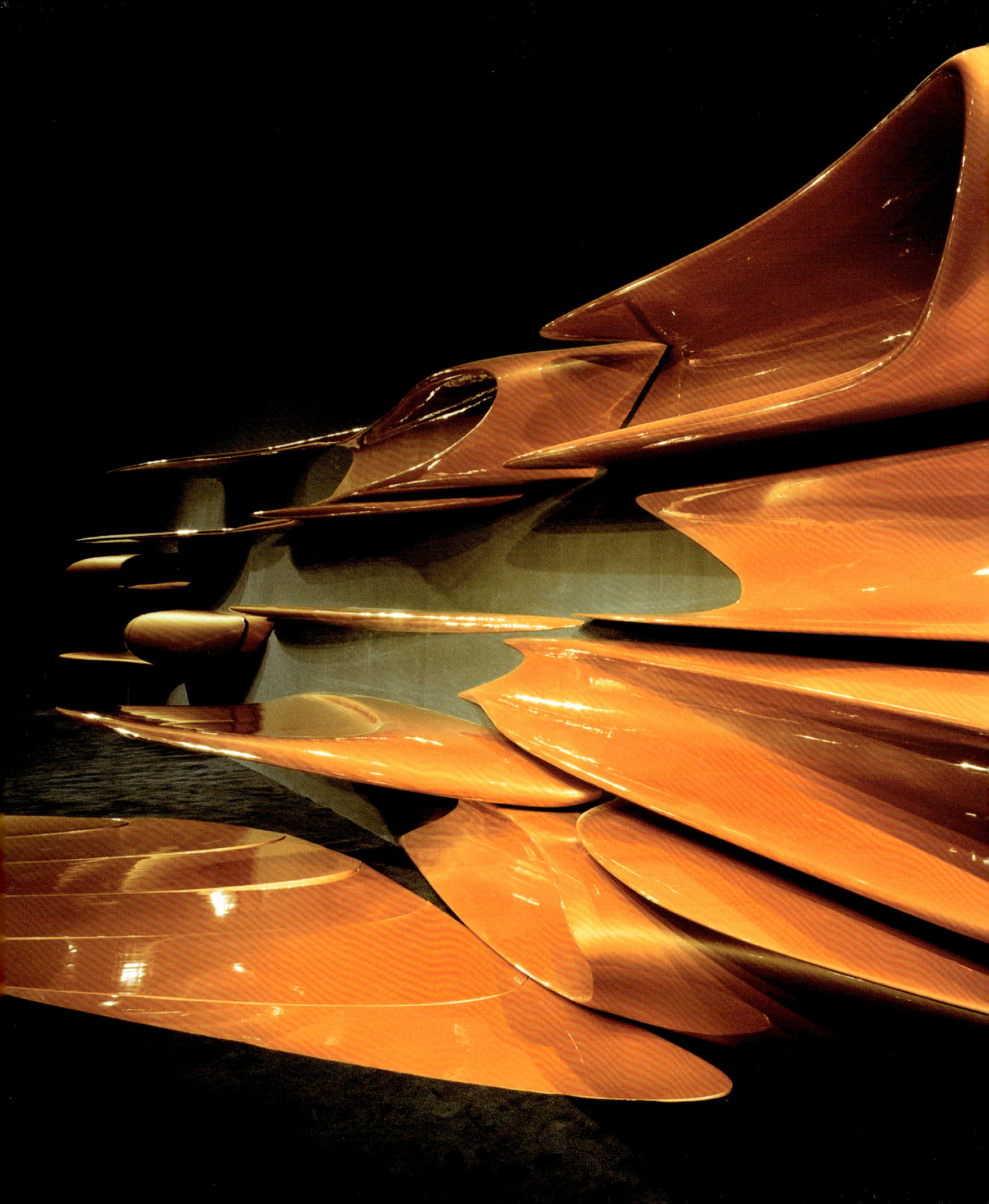

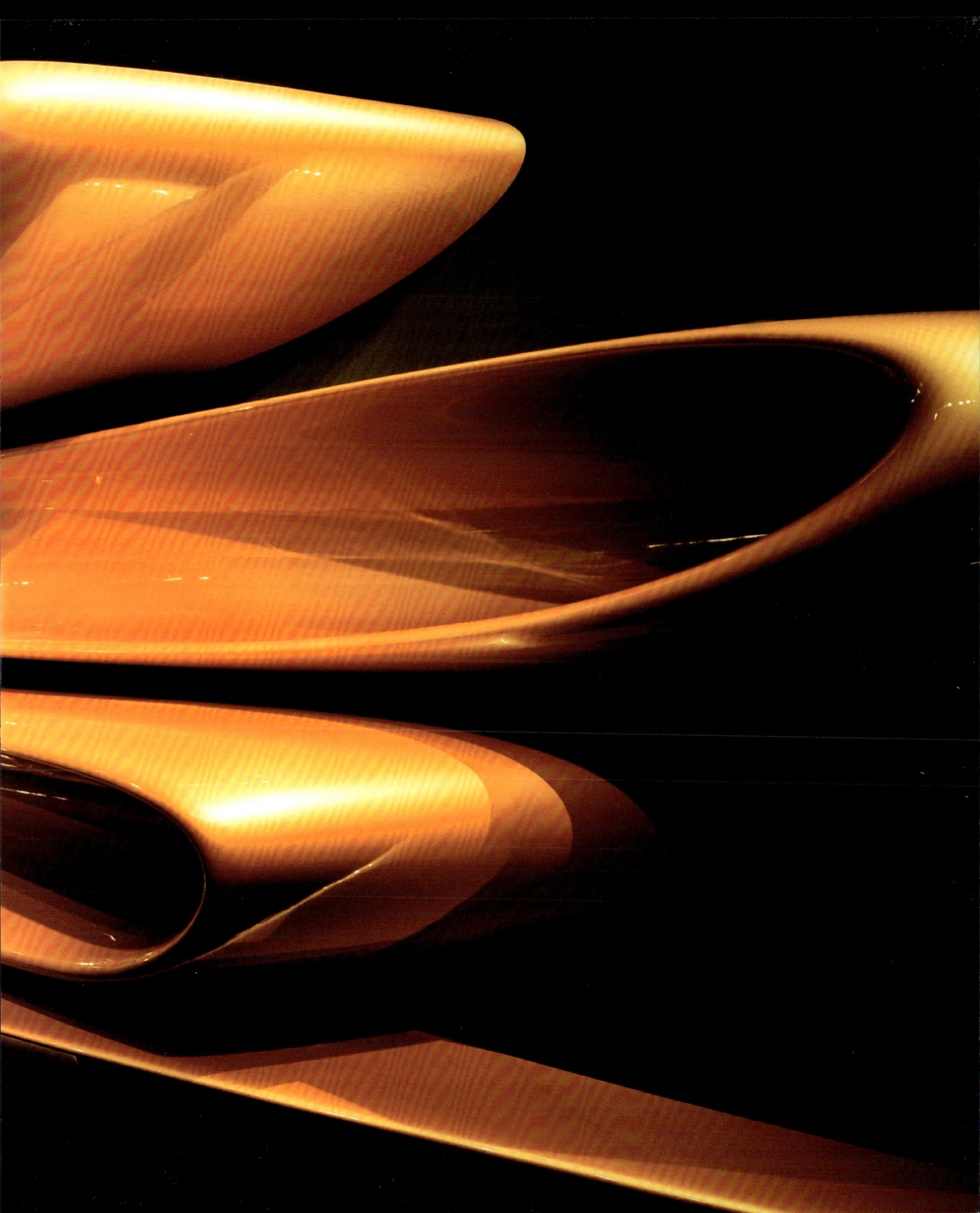

Cat. 3 (previous page)
Dune Formations **Furniture Elements** | 2007
Designed for David Gill Galleries
Aluminum, polyurethane resin, lacquer; W (*Dune 05* shelf) 157 ⅙" (399 cm)
Lent by David Gill Galleries

Dune Formations, an experimental series of some twenty furniture elements that includes tables, benches, wall shelving, and a tree-like standing shelf, began with London gallerist David Gill's brief to Hadid "to create a bookcase, a piece of furniture within her architectural strength that would obviously grow sideways, up and down."[1] The resulting units—vaguely parabolic in shape but individually varied as free-form volumes—are entirely unlike traditional shelves realized with two-dimensional geometry and standardized production. Hadid's most abstract furniture to date, the entire assemblage blends vertically and horizontally into continuous, curving, three-dimensional surfaces made possible by advanced computer modeling. The computer-generated shapes were produced as physical objects from a heat-molded composite of aluminum and polyurethane resin to which an orange lacquer finish (borrowed from the automobile industry) was applied. This sculptural furniture ensemble made its first appearance at the Venice Biennale in 2007, where it was installed at the Scuola dei Mercanti; it was subsequently shown at David Gill Galleries in London, and again by David Gill, in collaboration with Vista Art and Design, at Art Basel / Miami Beach 2010 in Miami. A silver version of *Dune Formations* was first shown at the 2008 Seoul Design Olympiad.

1. David Gill, quoted in "Vista Art and Design Present Zaha Hadid," 3:07, December 2010, http://www.artivi.com/vernissages/hadid.php.

Cat. 4
Mesa **Table** | 2007
Made by Vitra GmbH
Polyurethane base, fiberglass top, metallic paint finish; L 159 ⅙" (405 cm)
Lent by Vitra Design Museum, Weil am Rhein, Germany

Hadid's *Mesa* table was designed for Vitra Edition, a program launched by Vitra chairman Rolf Fehlbaum in 1987 to offer architects and designers creative freedom and technical support in the creation of experimental furniture and interior installations. The table evolved from Hadid's research into connecting physical and programmatic spaces for her design proposal for the Guggenheim Museum in Taichung, Taiwan (2003), and from her *Elastika* installation at Design Miami/Basel 2005 in Miami, where she zigzagged oblique, elongated beams across the multistoried central atrium of the Moore Building in Miami's Design District, visually connecting the floors by suggesting a continuity of structure. The same branching shapes are developed further in *Mesa*'s structural support system and in the Abu Dhabi Performing Arts Centre's (2007; fig. 6) skeletal frame of interconnecting steel tubes that support the building's structural glass curtain wall. Its title referencing the Spanish and Portuguese word for table as well as the flat-topped elevated landform, Hadid's large-scale *Mesa* table is supported by crisscrossing lofted connectors that define and divide the four flat sections of its surface into a continuous, nonlinear, self-supporting composition. The table was introduced by Vitra at Design Miami/Basel 2007 in Basel.

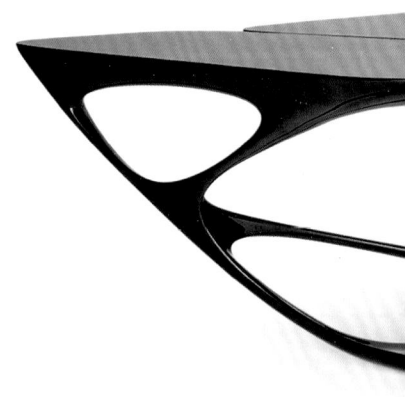

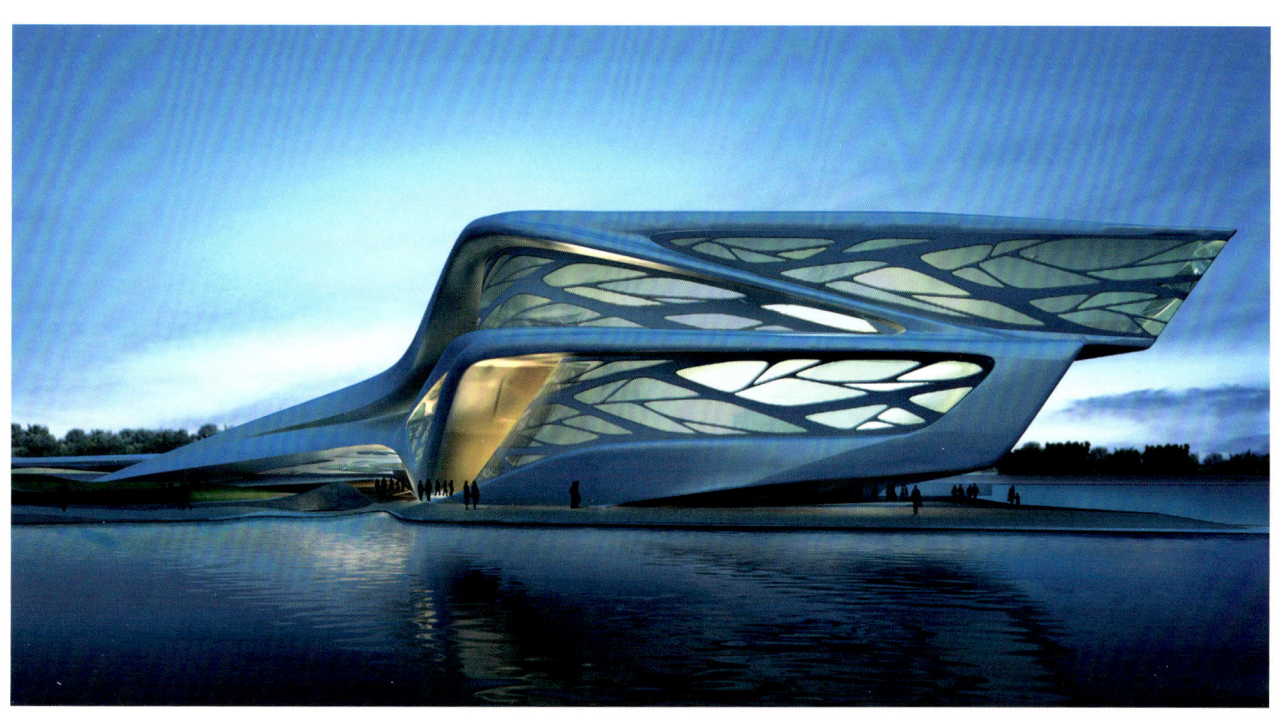

Fig. 6
Design for Abu Dhabi Performing Arts Centre (2007)
Courtesy Zaha Hadid Architects, London

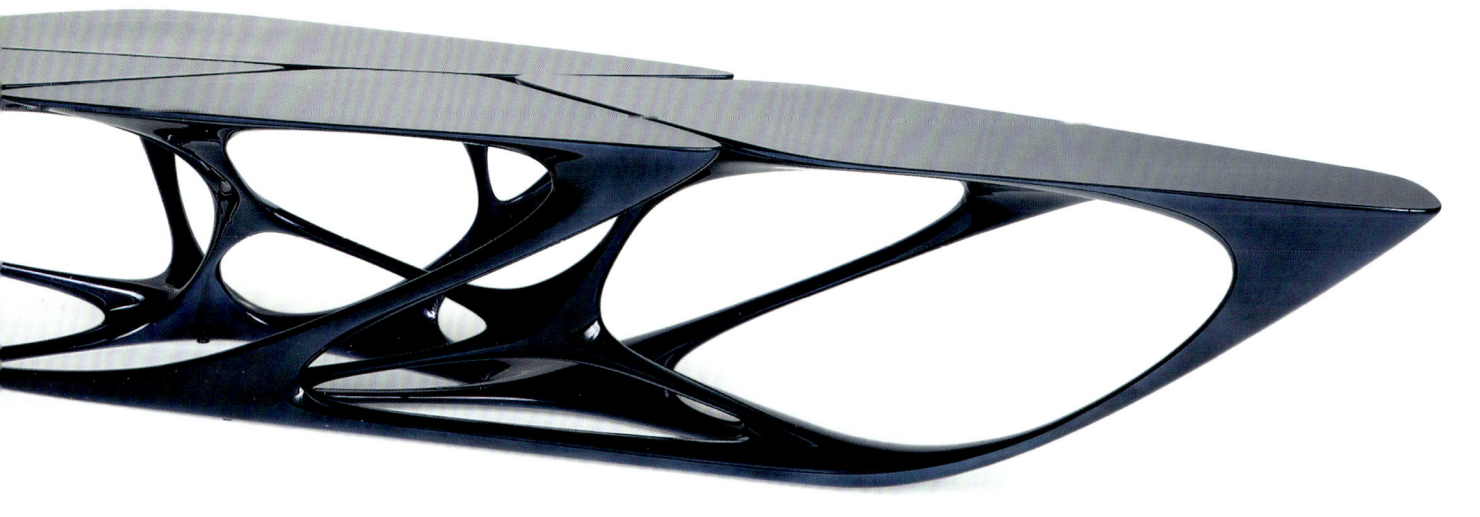

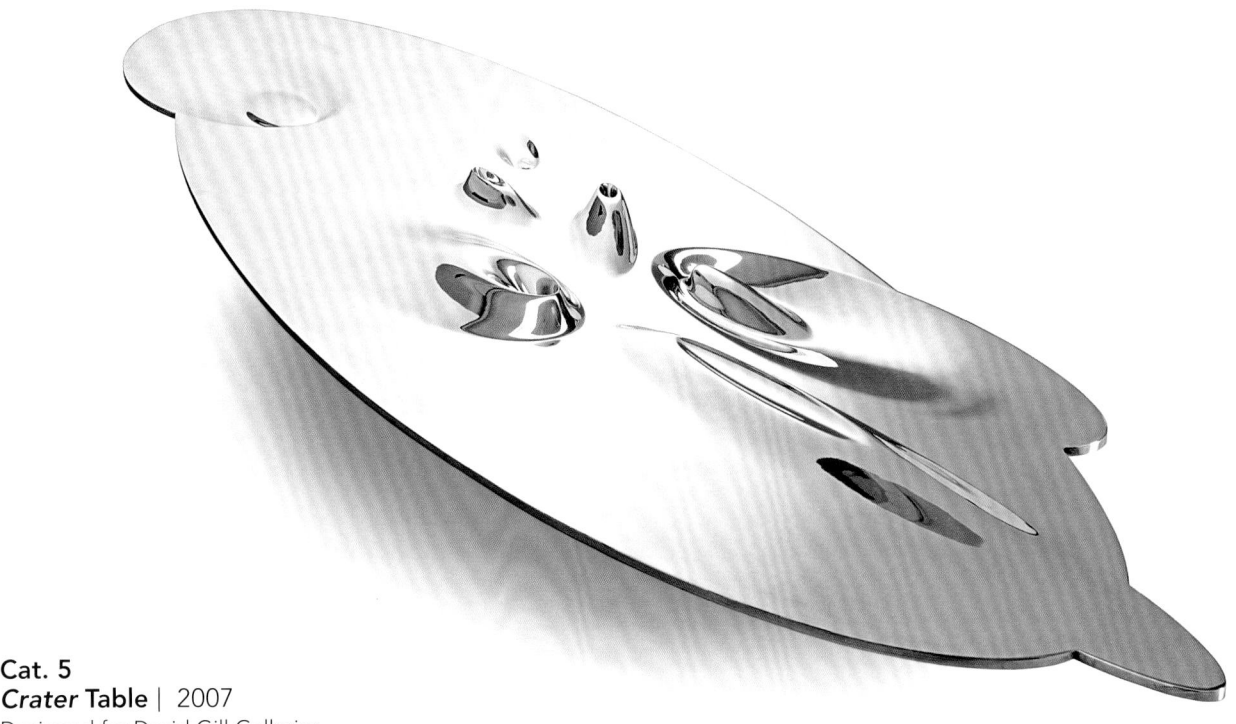

Cat. 5
Crater Table | 2007
Designed for David Gill Galleries
Aluminum with polished finish, L 104¾" (266 cm)
Lent by David Gill Galleries

Its sleek surface deformed with the volcano-like projections and bowl-shaped depressions that give the piece its name, *Crater* table has no precedent in the history of furniture. Ostensibly receptacles for food or display, like the depressions in the *Niche* centerpiece (see cat. 20), *Crater*'s disruptions test the limits of what distinguishes a table from the disparate objects placed on its surface. Two of the crater rims overhang the table's edge and extend toward the floor, providing the piece with support and balance. Varied in appearance, the craters reflect Hadid's interest in geomorphology and the tectonic forces that shape landforms into circular basins or conical summits, as well as her early and ongoing adoption of Russian Suprematist and Constructivist ideas, among them Kazimir Malevich's principle that motion is central to the treatment of form.[1] Its curving supports hidden underneath, the tabletop appears to be suspended in space, as do the lightweight roof structures of Hadid's Nordpark Railway Stations in Innsbruck, Austria (2004–7), which float on top of concrete plinths. Commissioned by London gallerist David Gill, the *Crater* table made its debut at Design Miami/Basel 2007 in Basel and was shown again in 2010 at the Galerie Gmurzynska in Zurich in the exhibition *Zaha Hadid and Suprematism*, which Hadid curated and designed.

1. See Kazimir Malevich, "Suprematism: 34 Drawings" (1920), reprinted in Patricia Railing, ed., *Malevich on Suprematism: Six Essays, 1915 to 1926* (Iowa City: University of Iowa Museum of Art, 1999), pp. 81–87.

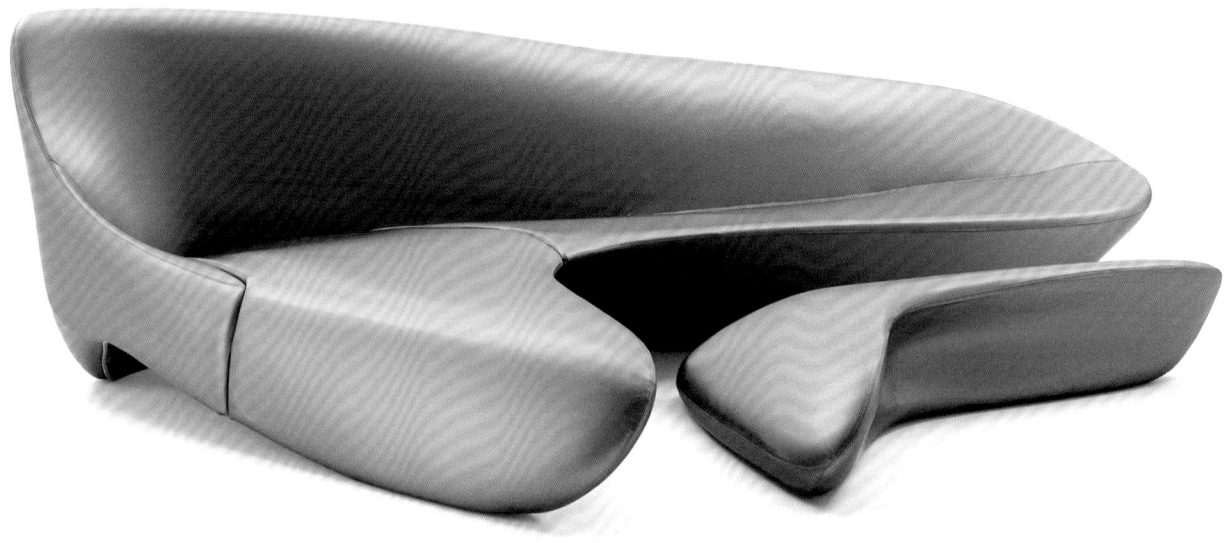

Cat. 6
Moon System **Sofa and Ottoman** | 2007
Made by B&B Italia
Steel, cold-pressed polyurethane foam, nylon/polyurethane/spandex upholstery
L (sofa) 113⅜" (288 cm), L (ottoman) 59 7/16" (151 cm)
Lent by B&B Italia

In the 1960s, B&B Italia pioneered cold-molding and the use of polyurethane with steel frames (instead of foam rubber with wooden armatures) to fabricate revolutionary upholstered seating such as Gaetano Pesce's *Up* series (1969). The company was similarly challenged by Hadid's complex, curvilinear geometries, which give the *Moon System* sofa and ottoman their unusual boomerang shape and thin profile. Circumscribed by a single, continuous dynamic line (into which the ottoman nests seamlessly), the *Moon System* sofa required B&B Italia for the first time to use a CNC milling machine, which shaped and cut the polyurethane foam as a single block containing the sofa's back, seat, and armrests according to the exact specifications of Hadid's three-dimensional computer model. This direct-to-production manufacturing technique allowed Hadid's original design concept—an assemblage of parts conceived as a singular production unit—to be fabricated with precision and economy of resource. The sofa was introduced at the Salone Internazionale del Mobile in Milan in spring 2008, where reviewers noted that *Moon*'s unique shape offers users a variety of comfortable seating possibilities.

Cat. 7
Kloris **Seating Elements** | 2008
Designed for and in collaboration with Julian A. Treger and Kenny Schachter / Rove Projects LLP
Glass-reinforced plastic with high-gloss lacquer finish, steel base plates; L 255 ⅞" (650 cm)
Lent by Kenny Schachter / Rove Projects LLP

This cluster of ten sculptural seating elements, composed as individually shaped, abstract flower petals, is named after the classical Greek word for yellowish or pale green. *Kloris* was designed and made for *Beyond Limits*, Sotheby's exhibition of modern and contemporary outdoor sculpture held in fall 2008 in the vast gardens of Chatsworth, one of Britain's most splendid historic houses. Made of fiberglass glossily finished in gradations of green and chrome to blend with and reflect its landscape site, *Kloris* was commissioned by Kenny Schachter of Rove Projects, London, in collaboration with the collector Julian A. Treger. As the Chatsworth exhibition closed, Schachter showed this all-chrome version of *Kloris* in New York in the two-venue exhibition *Zaha Hadid* he organized for and with Sonnabend Gallery. Including examples of Hadid's art, design, and architecture, the exhibition demonstrated the interrelation of these disciplines in her practice and the resulting hybrid nature of works such as *Kloris*. Each element of this seat sculpture was digitally designed and fabricated: the free-form shapes were generated as three-dimensional digital models with CAD tools; rapid-prototyped into physical models for review and refinement; and then developed, with CAM software, into CNC-milled polyurethane foam molds in which the fiberglass forms finally were cast. Offering unprecedented formal freedom, these advanced technologies also promote new collaborative strategies for Hadid and her engineers.

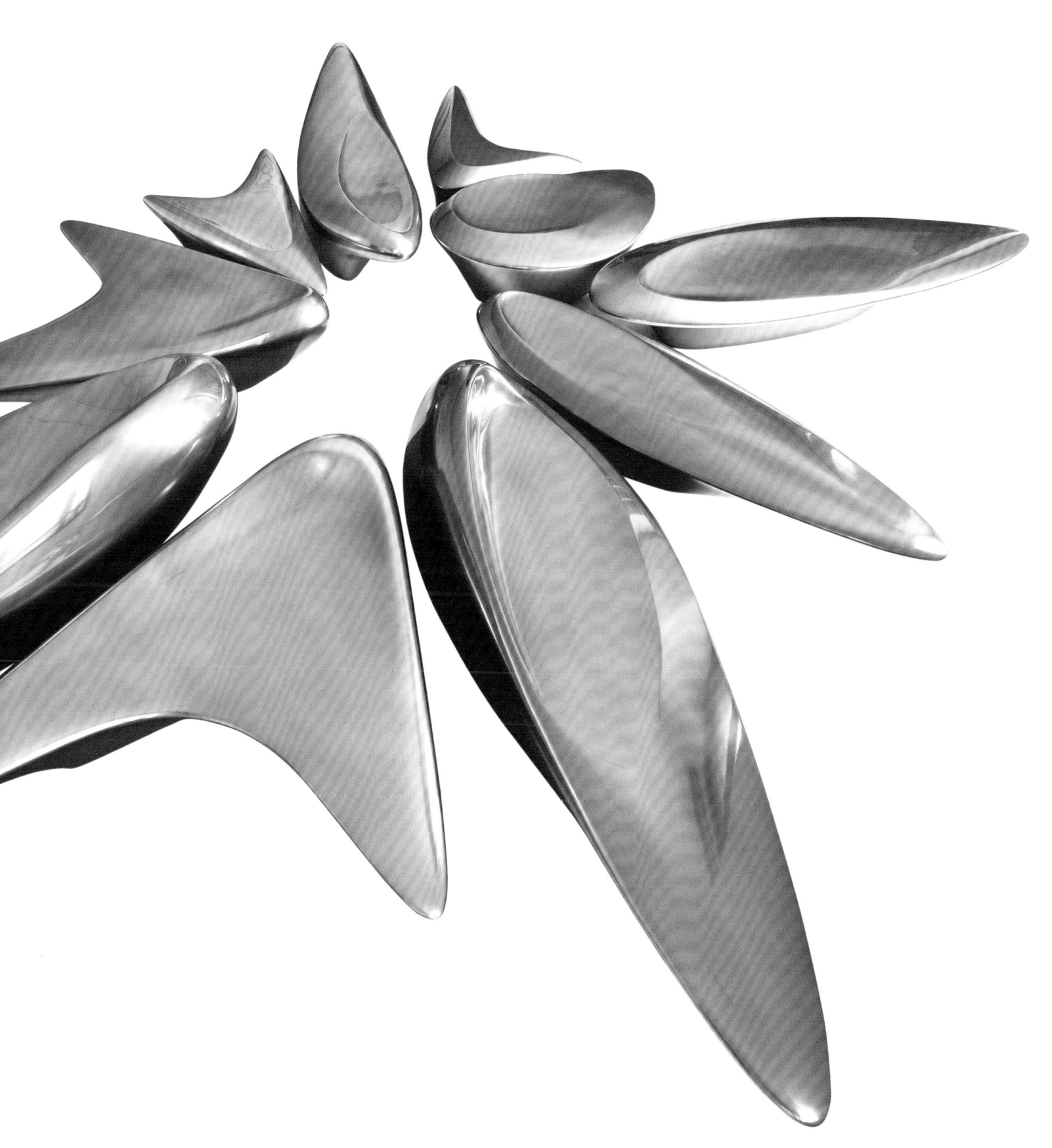

Cat. 8
Zephyr Sofa | 2010
Designed for Zaha Hadid Architects
Lacquered fiberglass, polyurethane-coated polyester upholstery; L 111 ⅞" (284 cm)
Lent by Zaha Hadid Architects

This fragmented, double-sided sofa with abstract, patterned upholstery on one side based on Hadid's 1982–83 competition-winning entry for The Peak, Hong Kong (see fig. 7), was shown for the first time at the exhibition *Zaha Hadid and Suprematism*, held at the Galerie Gmurzynska in Zurich in June–September 2010. This exhibition was the first to juxtapose her work with that of the Russian avant-garde artist-theorists central to her writing, teaching, and practice since her student days. Hadid, who organized the exhibition according to four Suprematist pictorial devices (abstraction, distortion, fragmentation, and flotation—concepts that could all be applied to this sofa), still finds in Suprematism "a major source of inspiration. Fragmentation of image is still an excellent way to interpret context, just as abstraction is when observing and creating an object."[1] Reprising elements of the cantilevered, boomerang-shaped "woosh" sofa she designed for William Bitar in 1985–86, which featured two separate upholstery treatments and backrests, the *Zephyr*, like the earlier sofa, appears to levitate while seating "two or ten"[2] people simultaneously.

1. "La mostra sul Suprematismo a Zurigo / The Exhibition on Suprematism in Zurich,"
in "Being Zaha Hadid," special issue, *Abitare*, no. 511 (April 2011), p. 89.
2. Deborah K. Dietsch, "A Room of One's Own: Living Room Suite, London,"
Architectural Record, vol. 175, no. 11 (September 1987), p. 87.

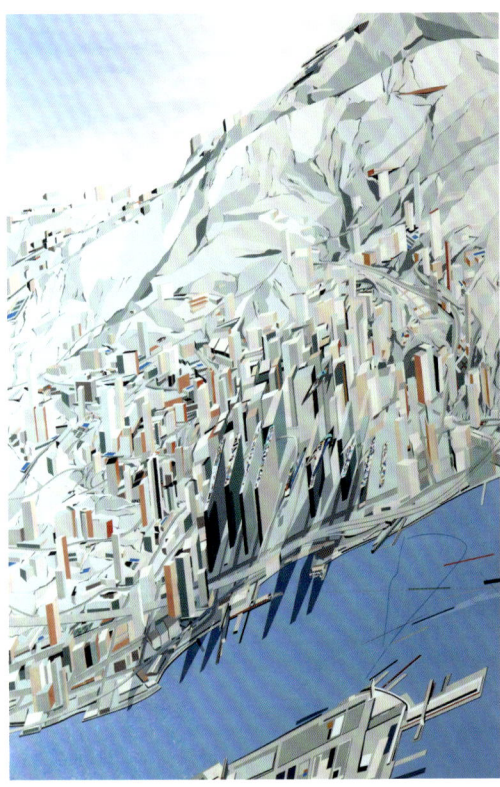

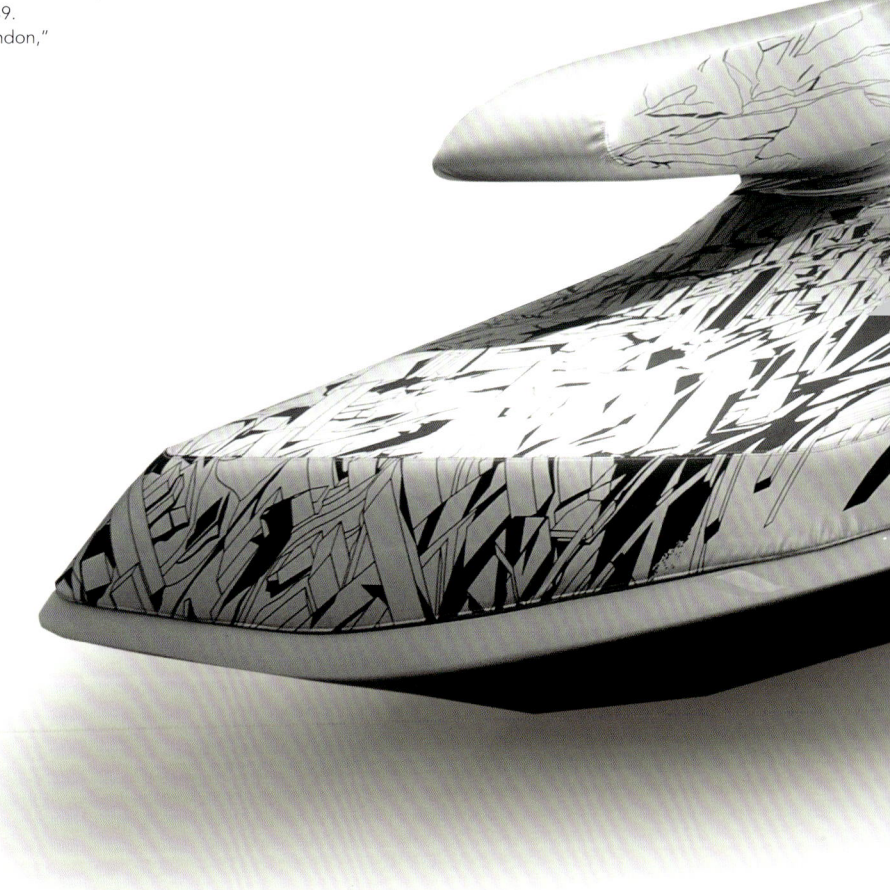

Fig. 7
Zaha Hadid, *The Blue Slabs*, painting for
The Peak, Hong Kong (1982–83)
Courtesy Zaha Hadid Architects, London

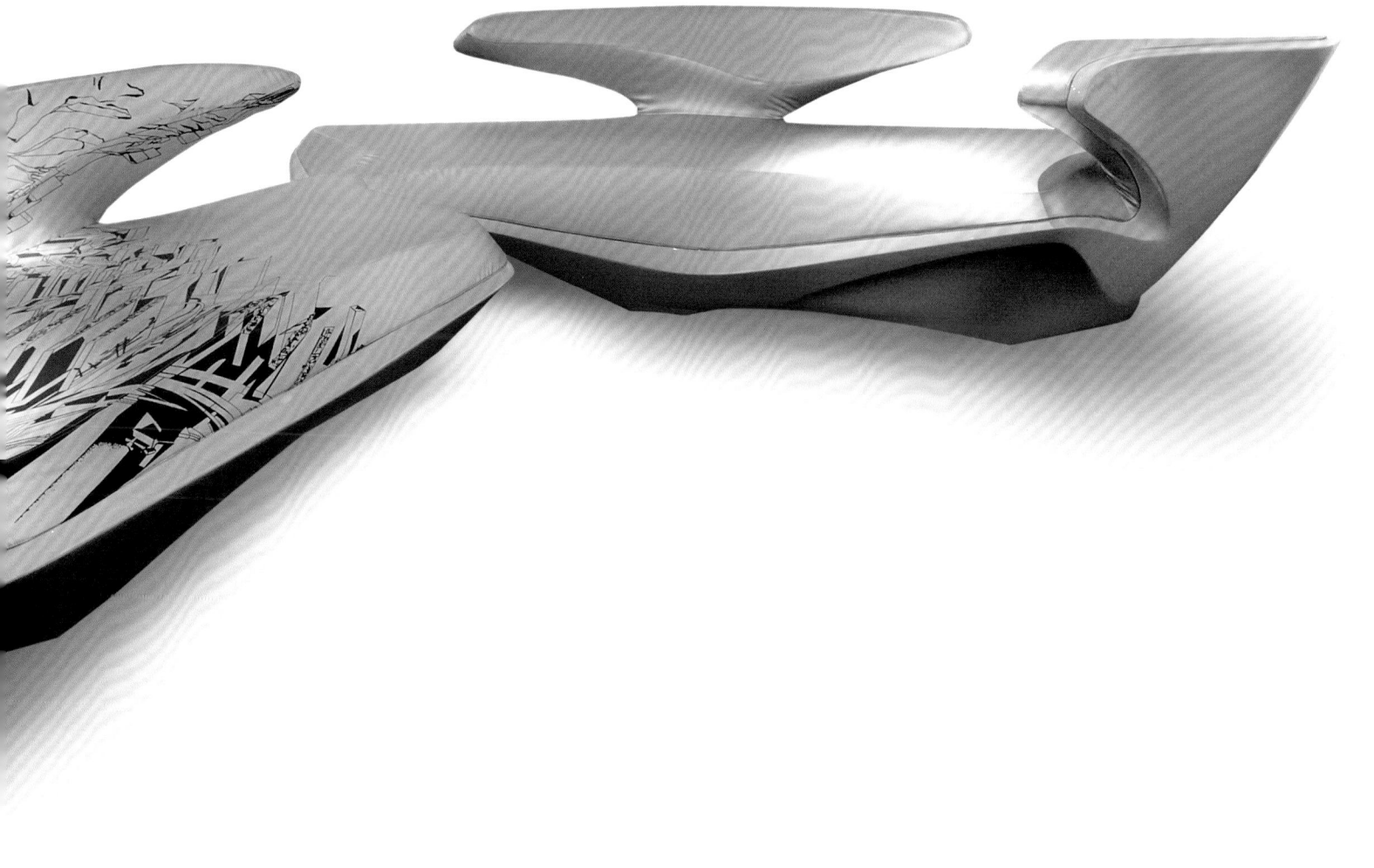

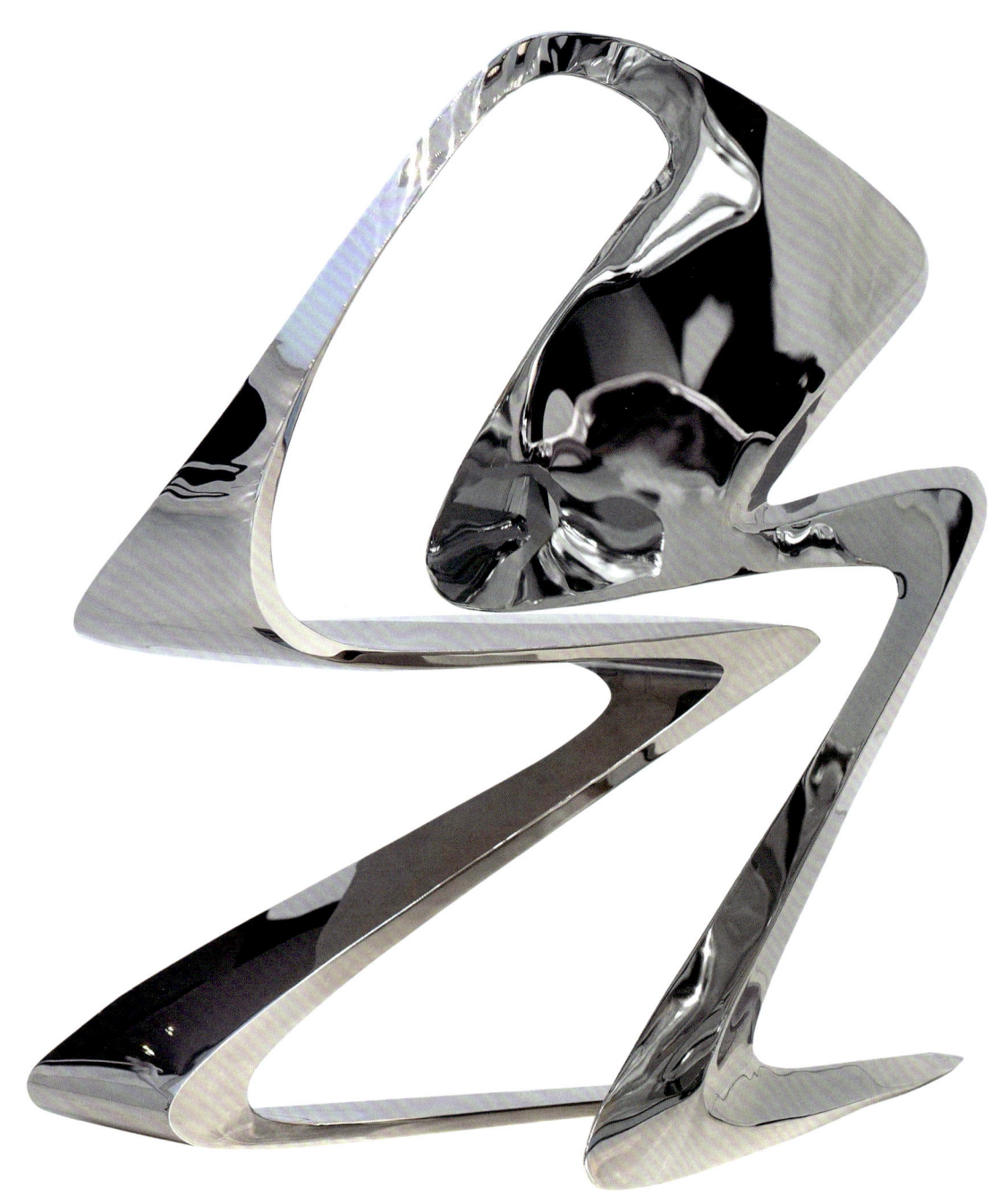

Cat. 9
Z-Chair | 2011
Made by Sawaya & Moroni
Stainless steel, H 34 ⅝" (88 cm)
Lent by Sawaya & Moroni

Like the zigzagging, zinc-clad roof line of Hadid's recently completed Riverside Museum of Transport in Glasgow (2004–11; fig. 8), the profile of the *Z-Chair* is strongly gestural, capturing the architect's fluid, calligraphic hand more directly than her other design objects. Reprising the angular corners of her earliest work, Hadid contrasts these lines with the wide, smooth, curving surfaces of the chair's seat and back. The *Z-Chair* was launched at Milan's Salone Internazionale del Mobile in April 2011, heir to a distinguished historical progression of cantilevered chairs that aspired to single-piece construction, from Gerrit Rietveld's wooden *ZigZag* chair of 1932–33 to Verner Panton's molded fiberglass-reinforced polyester chair of 1960–67 (which Hadid uses in the meeting rooms of her office and celebrated in her *Hommage à Verner Panton* drawing for Vitra in 1990). Made of resilient, polished stainless steel, the *Z-Chair* gives the impression of having been fabricated from a single, continuous loop of metal, thickened at the heels and back for structural support, and given additional visual unity by its highly reflective surface. In fact, the chair was laser-cut and hammered by hand into shape over a CNC-milled wooden framework.

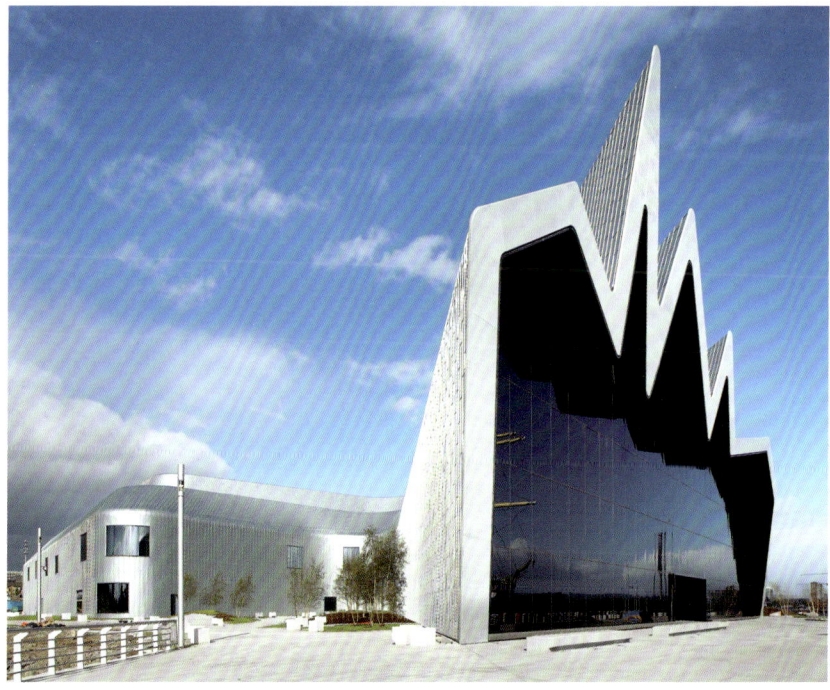

Fig. 8
Riverside Museum of Transport, Glasgow (2004–11)
Photograph by Hufton + Crow
Courtesy Zaha Hadid Architects, London

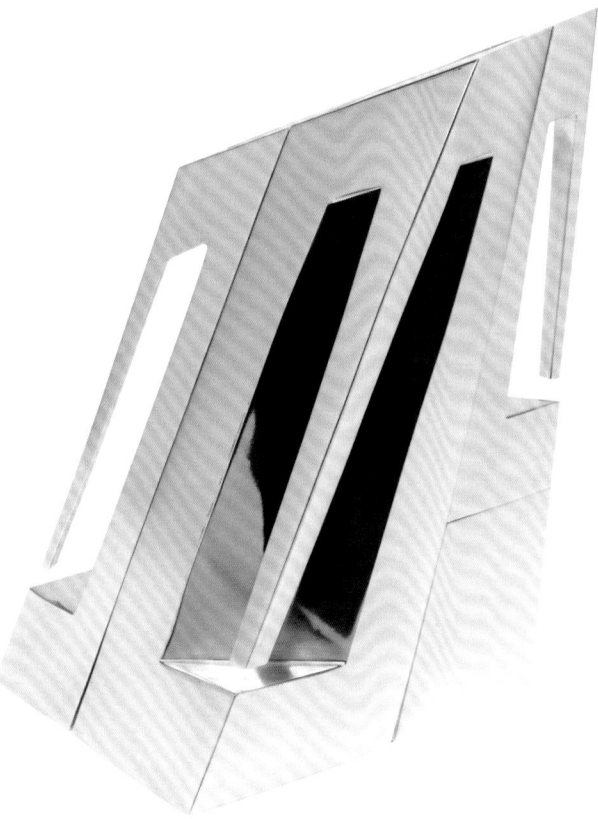

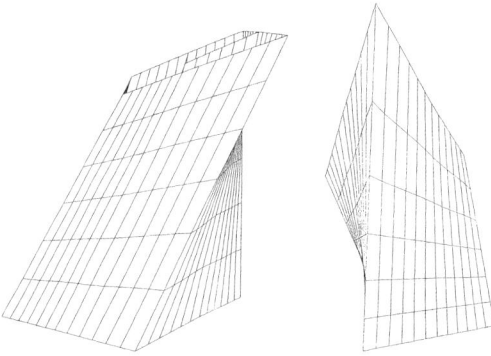

Fig. 9
Computer perspective of
Sawaya & Moroni tea and coffee service, 1996
Courtesy Zaha Hadid Architects, London

Cat. 10
Tea and Coffee Service | 1995–96
Made by Sawaya & Moroni
Silver, H (coffeepot) 11" (28 cm)
Lent by Sawaya & Moroni

William Sawaya and Paolo Moroni have distinguished their company through collaborations with international architects and designers, producing furniture, accessories, and silver. Hadid's limited-edition tea and coffee service for Sawaya & Moroni was one of her first design objects to be produced. Raised out of welded sheets hammered into shape in Sawaya & Moroni's silversmithing workshop, the service consists of four pieces—teapot, coffeepot, sugar bowl, and milk jug—that can be assembled as a table sculpture or separated according to function. Unlike Hadid's later digitally generated and prototyped designs, this set was realized from a drawing, albeit one based on abstract spatial mapping and projective geometry (figs. 9, 10). The highly polished, sharp-edged, prismatic forms of the service tilt off square, reflecting Hadid's ongoing research of tall buildings as segments with different directional movements. As in her then recently completed Vitra Fire Station in Weil am Rhein, Germany (1990–94), Hadid treats the surfaces of these vessels like vertical tectonic plates that come to sharp points and appear to slide together or past each other in a state of frozen motion, applying her extensive study of geological formations, materials, and forces as she has throughout her creative work, whether architecture, design, sculpture, or painting.

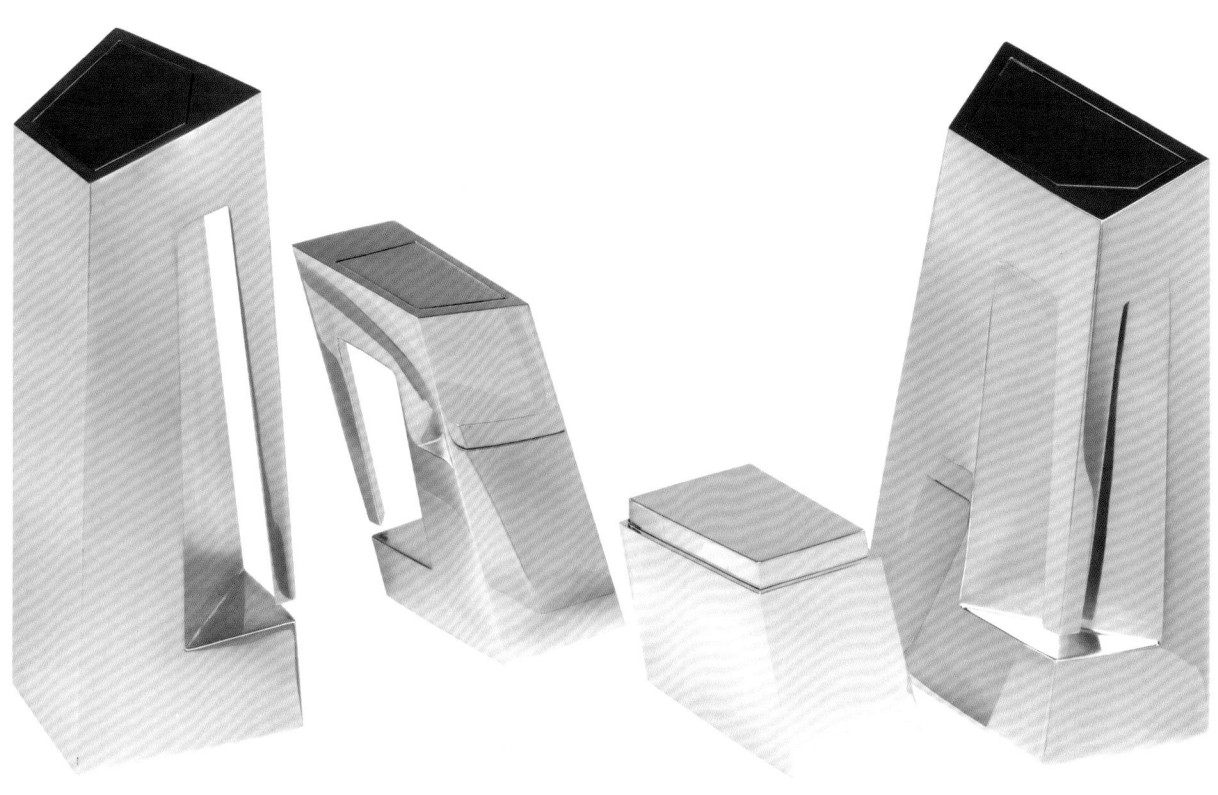
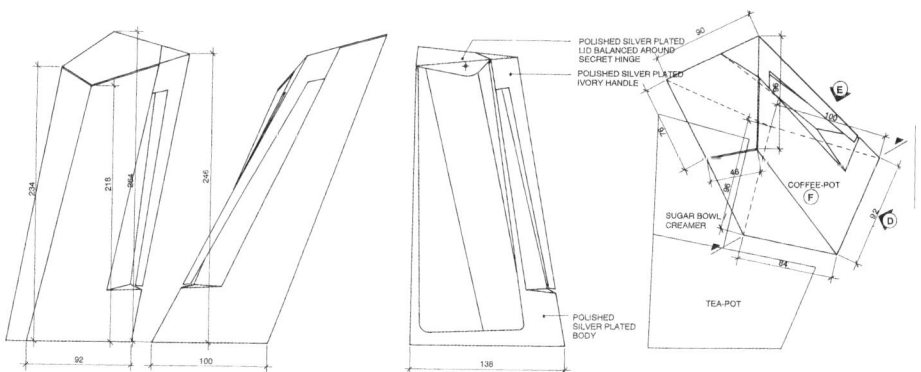

Fig. 10
Elevations, section, and plan of
Sawaya & Moroni coffeepot, 1996
Courtesy Zaha Hadid Architects, London

Cat. 11
Z-Car I | 2005–6
Designed for and in collaboration with Kenny Schachter / Rove Projects LLP
High-density polyurethane foam with pearlescent finish, L 149 ⅜" (380 cm)
Lent by Kenny Schachter / Rove Projects LLP

Conceived by Kenny Schachter, principal of Rove Projects, London, as the first in a series of concept cars designed by "an artist, architect or other creative type,"[1] the *Z-Car* made its debut in the 2006 *Zaha Hadid* exhibition at the Solomon R. Guggenheim Museum, New York. Another model was also shown at the British International Motor Show in London the same summer. While developing the car with Hadid, Schachter also commissioned from her a mixed-use building in Hoxton, East London; "a furniture-sculpture-storage object"[2] that he showed in 2006 at the ARCO fine art fair in Madrid and again at the Guggenheim exhibition; and the *Belu* bench, a multifunctional furniture form first shown at Design Miami/Basel in 2007. When potential manufacturers questioned the vehicle's roadworthiness, Schachter responded: "Roadworthiness is less important than getting it made at all. I look on the car and the building I'm doing with Zaha as sculptures. Hopefully we can produce a few cars like art editions with the minimum of compromise, but if not, the process has still been cool."[3] This first version of the *Z-Car*, which could be powered by an electric motor or hydrogen fuel cell, is a three-wheeled, two-seat compact automobile designed for the challenges of urban driving and parking. Its aerodynamic, streamlined shape and asymmetrical windscreen-door—which, like the DeLorean DMC-12's gull-wing, swings up to allow passenger access—reflect Hadid's characteristic formal language. New carbon fiber materials that are strong and lightweight are intended to achieve these structural curves, as they did initially in the aerospace industry. The first *Z-Car* prototype was succeeded in 2008 by a four-wheeled model that was included in the 2011 *Car Culture* exhibition at the Zentrum für Kunst und Medientechnologie, Karlsruhe, Germany. No working models of the *Z-Car* have been built to date.

1. Kenny Schachter, "Art Dealer's Diary," *Modern Magazine*, July 26, 2006, www.artnet.com/magazineus/features/schachter/schachter7-26-06.asp.
2. Ibid.
3. "Kenny Schachter: Confessions of an Art Hustler," *The Independent*, June 25, 2006, http://www.independent.co.uk/news/people/profiles. Kenny-Schachter-confessions-of-an-art-hustler-405194.html.

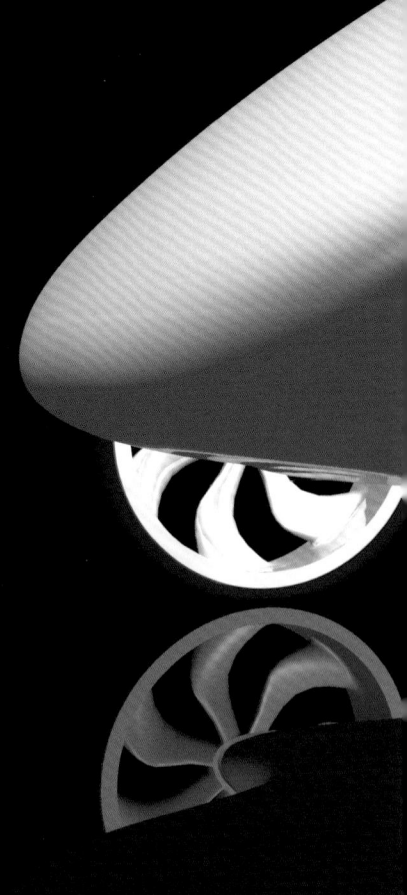

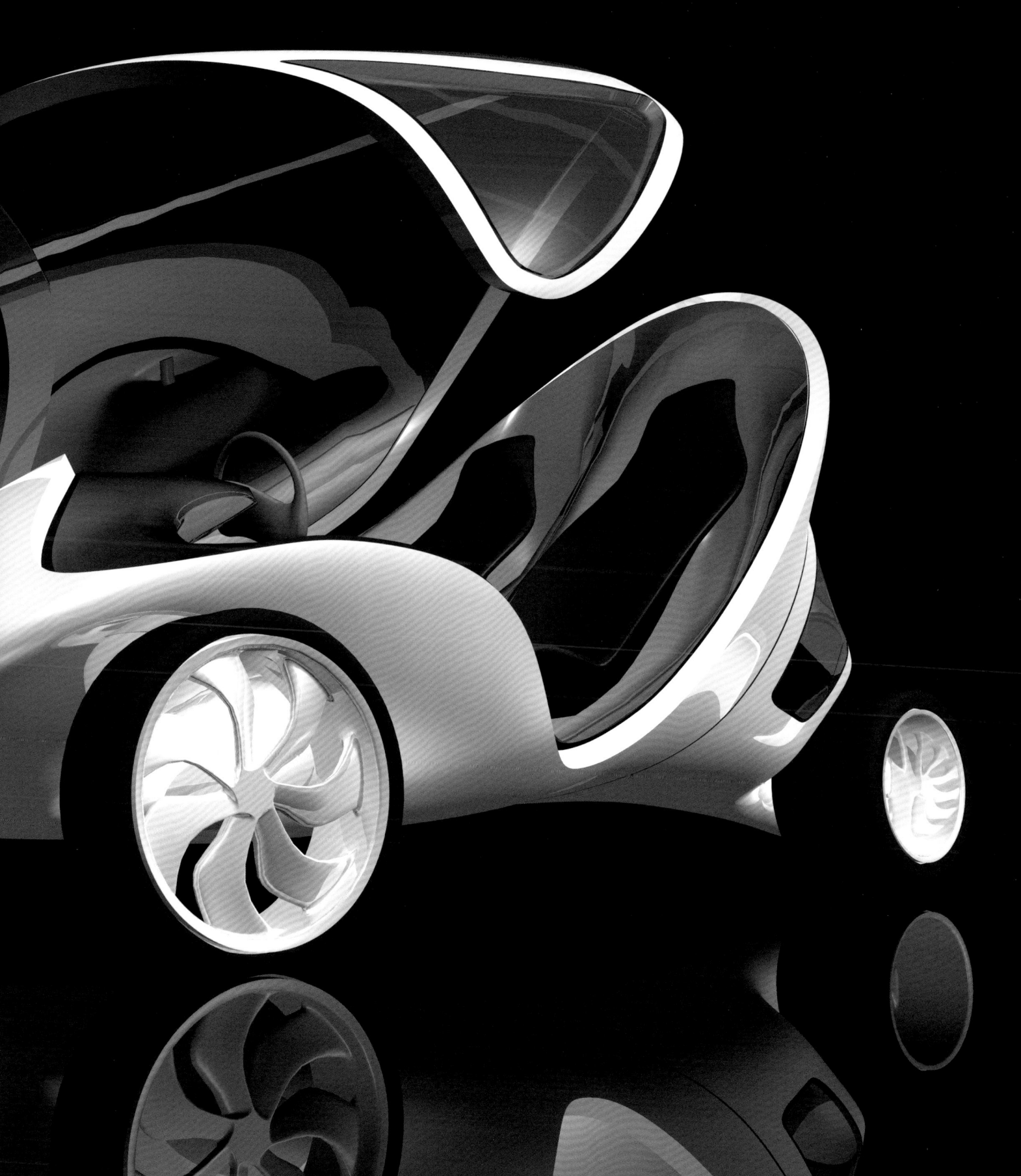

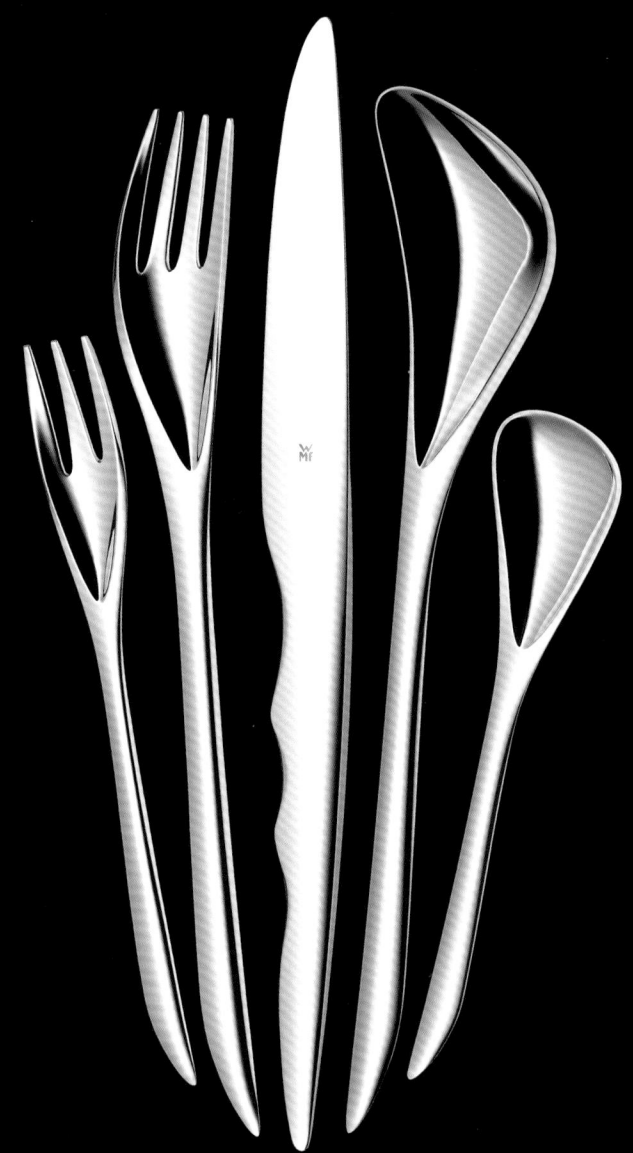

Cat. 12
Flatware | 2007
Made by WMF, Württembergische Metallwarenfabrik AG
Stainless steel, L (table knife) 9 ⅝" (24.5 cm)
Philadelphia Museum of Art. Gift of Lisa S. Roberts, 2007-106-2–6

Departing from traditional cutlery shapes such as oval spoon bowls and straight, parallel-sided handles, all five pieces in this curvilinear place setting—table fork, table knife, tablespoon, dessert fork, and teaspoon—are asymmetrical and different in profile. The forks and spoons have scoop-shaped bowls that are thinner, straighter, and flatter at one edge, allowing the diner to capture small pieces of food and scrape the last morsel from the plate with ease. The wave-sided knife handle's depressions fit comfortably to the diner's fingers. Combining ergonomic concerns with the accelerated curves used in car design, Hadid generated these unique shapes with computational tools, particularly software that allows three-dimensional rendering of nonrepeating geometries and manufacturing of complex, curving surfaces. A project study for the flatware was included in the 2006 *Zaha Hadid* exhibition at the Solomon R. Guggenheim Museum, New York.

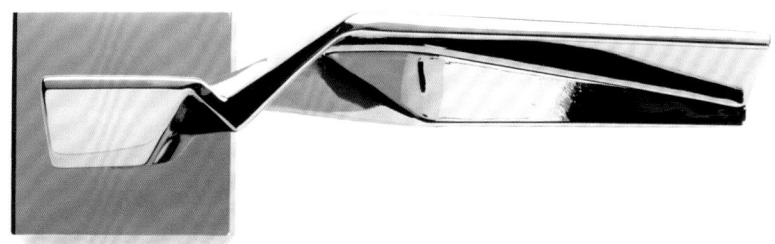

Cat. 13
Fusital **Door Handle** | 2007
Made by Valli & Valli
Brass, Nikrall Zamak alloy; L 6 ¾" (17.1 cm)
Lent by Valli & Valli USA, a division of ASSA ABLOY

Zaha Hadid's discussions with Italian hardware manufacturer Valli & Valli concerning a project for the company's Fusital line of designer products began in 1996 and continued for nearly a decade. Valli & Valli received Hadid's first project proposal in 2001. Her door handle design, which features an angular downward crimp, took four years to engineer and fabricate before making its debut at the Salone Internazionale del Mobile in Milan in spring 2005. One problem Valli & Valli faced was finding a material that could be die cast into such a complex shape; the company eventually chose a zinc aluminum alloy known for its strength and hardness that can be finished handsomely with chrome. While Valli & Valli continued its fabrication experiments, Hadid was designing the first floor of guest rooms in the Hotel Puerta America in Madrid (2003–5) that would feature other floors by distinguished architects and designers, including Ron Arad, Norman Foster, Arata Isozaki, and Jean Nouvel. Hadid's door handles were eventually installed in the hallways of the first-floor rooms, where they share the design language of complex, dynamic forms she employed within.

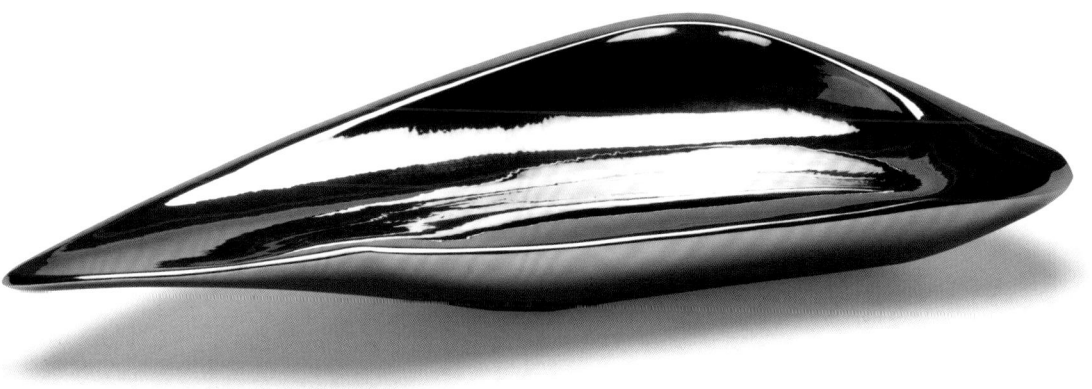

Cat. 14
Bowl | 2007
Made by Sawaya & Moroni
Silver, W 23 ⅝" (60 cm)
Lent by Sawaya & Moroni

A dozen years after her tea and coffee service was created in association with Sawaya & Moroni (see cat. 10), a new collaboration for bowls produced in metacrylic and silver revealed the evolution of Hadid's formal language and the advancement of three-dimensional design software, which has enabled her to create the complex, curving, fluid shapes that have since characterized her work. Concave in its center, the free-form volume of this bowl was derived from that of seating elements Hadid had earlier designed for Sawaya (*Z-Scape*, 2000), as well as from her proposals for the BBC Music Centre in London and the Guggenheim Museum in Taichung, Taiwan (both 2003). Like these projects, the bowl emphasizes horizontal movement with an overhanging prow, but smoothes the multiple transitions into a single continuous flow.

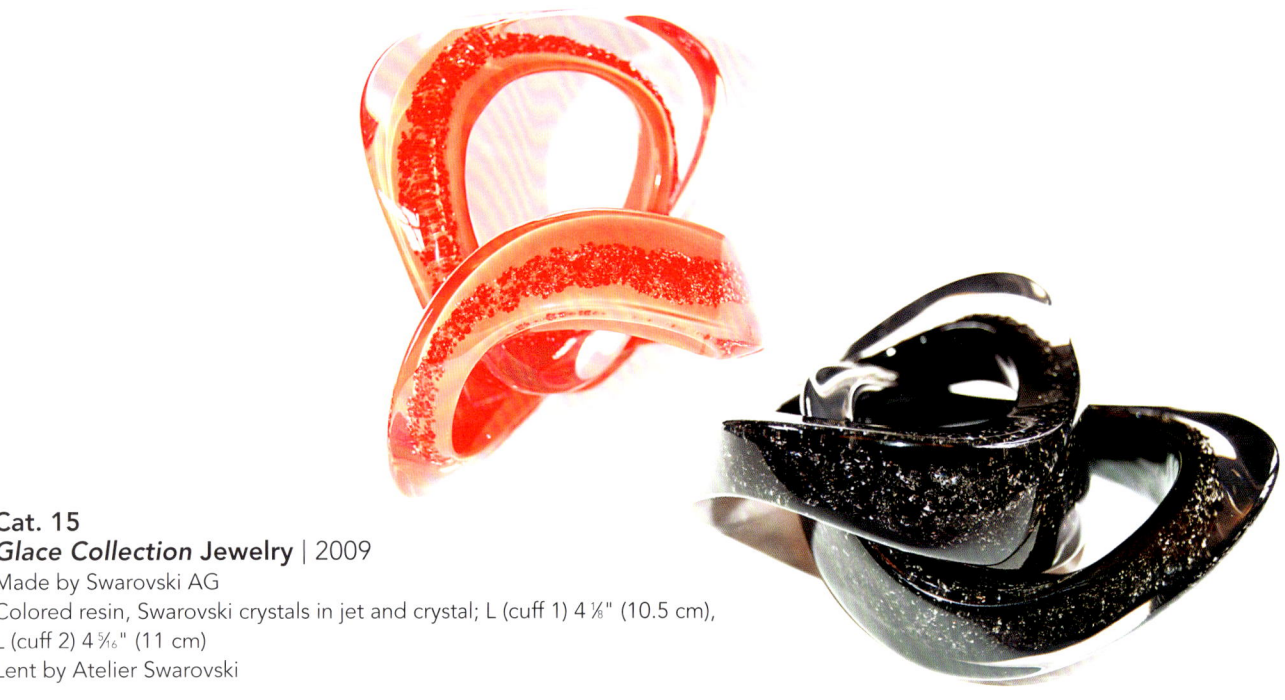

Cat. 15
Glace Collection **Jewelry** | 2009
Made by Swarovski AG
Colored resin, Swarovski crystals in jet and crystal; L (cuff 1) 4 ⅛" (10.5 cm),
L (cuff 2) 4 5/16" (11 cm)
Lent by Atelier Swarovski

Cat. 16
Celeste **Necklace** | 2008
Made by Swarovski AG
Made with Swarovski gemstones in topaz white, smoky quartz, and black spinel;
blackened silver; L 16 15/16" (43 cm)
Lent by Swarovski Runway Rocks

Hadid's collaboration with Swarovski, luxury producer of lead crystal objects, jewelry, and lighting, has resulted in necklaces, cuff bracelets, rings, and a floor-to-ceiling chandelier of cable-strung crystals introduced at the Salone Internazionale del Mobile in Milan in 2008. Combining crystals, precious stones, silver, and resin, the jewelry reflects Hadid's preoccupation with fluid forms that bend and torque seamlessly in apparent continuous movement. Devoid of clasps and closures, the *Glace* bracelets form asymmetrical, continuous loops that can be interlocked by means of embedded magnets. They are designed by three-dimensional computer-generated modeling wherein digitized ribbons are combined and manipulated into directional flows through advanced mathematical calculation. Swarovski then uses the computer model file to produce detailed molds into which the resin is poured; as the poured resin gradually hardens, crystals and stones are selectively suspended in it. Hadid also supplied Swarovski with a book of drawings showing multiple ways in which the *Glace Collection* jewelry can be worn. The silver *Celeste* necklace is similarly designed and cast according to curvilinear geometries that follow the form of the individual wearing it; the necklace rises from the wearer's torso, wraps around her neck, and comes to rest on her shoulder. Its accompanying cuff extends along the length of the forearm, continuing the formal movement of the composition. Moving away from the static limitations of Euclidian geometry and Cartesian coordinate systems, Hadid has capitalized on emerging technologies to achieve similarly looping, curvilinear shapes throughout her work, as in her design for the "Tap of the Future" for Triflow (2009), which emulates the flow of water through a faucet.

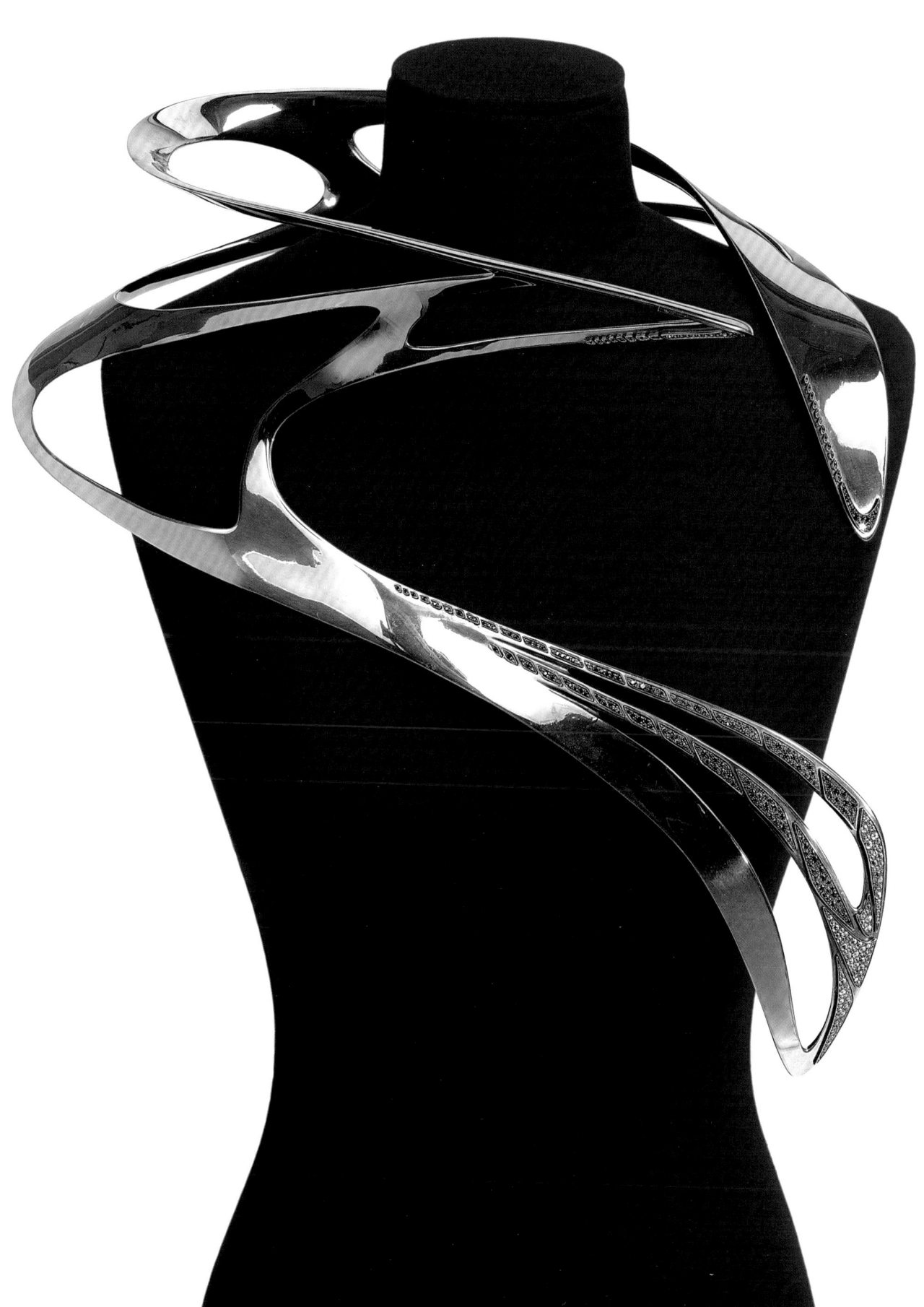

Cat. 17
Melissa **Shoes** | 2008
Made by Grendene S.A.
Mold-injected plastic, L (women's size 9) 10" (25.4 cm)
Lent by Melissa Shoes

These limited-edition strapped plastic shoes for Melissa, a brand of the Brazilian footwear company Grendene, mark Hadid's first venture into fashion design. Melissa's collaborations with well-known architects and designers—among them Vivienne Westwood, Gaetano Pesce, Karim Rashid, and the Campana Brothers—have given the label a reputation for highly styled and innovative designs. The company's eco-friendly, recyclable shoes are made of mold-injected PVC, EVA, and other synthetic fabrics.[1] Hadid's complex curved design was produced using advanced three-dimensional computer modeling and prototyping that could be combined directly with Melissa's molding process.[2] Highly organic in form, with diagonally sloping straps framing open spaces, the shoe's contours pour over and around the wearer's foot and ankle.

1. "Vivienne Westwood Collaborates with Brazilian Company Melissa,"
Melissa Shoes, accessed July 8, 2011, http://melissashoes.org/vivienne-westwood.
2. The three-dimensional computer modeling was done on NURBS-based
programs such as RhinoCAD, Maya, and 3ds Max.

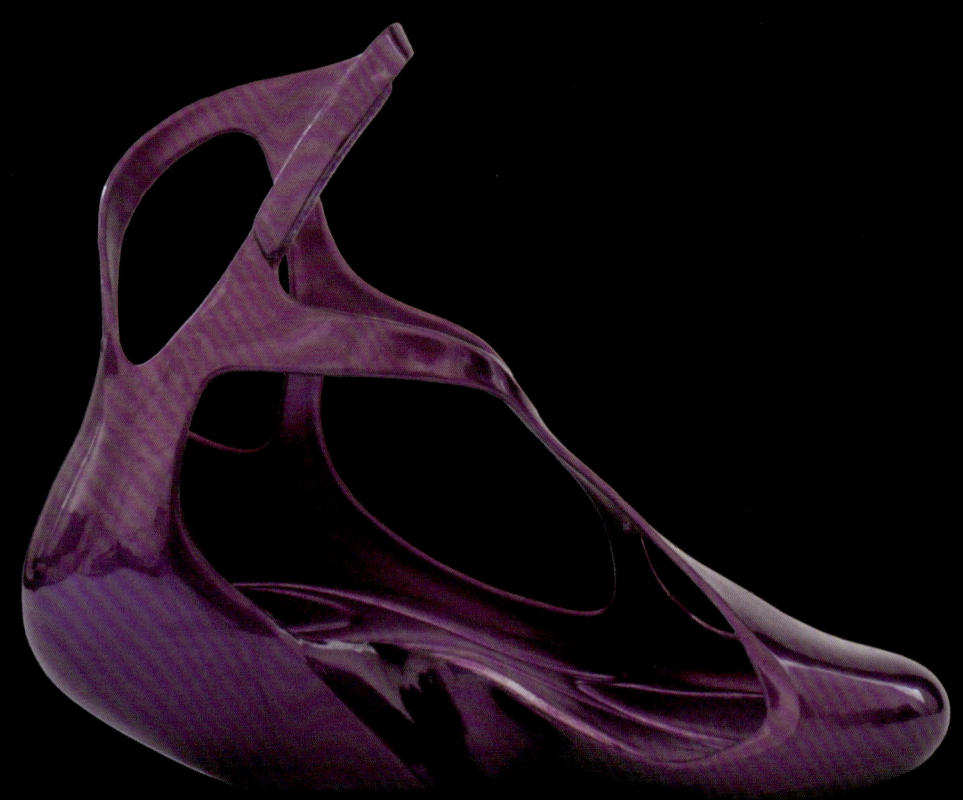

Cat. 18
Zaha Hadid Limited Edition Footwear | 2009
Made by Lacoste S.A.
Leather, rubber; various sizes
Lent by Lacoste Footwear

The crocodile pattern embossed on these leather shoes for Lacoste parallels the use of pattern in Hadid's more recent architectural work, such as her design for the Stone Towers development in Cairo (2008), which, in contrast to the sleek, reflective exterior surfaces that typically distinguish Hadid's buildings, utilizes precast façade patterns derived from minarets and Egyptian hieroglyphics to emulate the textural effects of light and shadow on traditional Egyptian stonework. Departing from the crocodile logo with which the Lacoste brand is so famously identified, Hadid created a digitized pattern based on the crocodile's scaly, armored skin with its shadowy depressions and reflective protrusions, similar to the seamless, fluid forms and scale-like patterning on the glass fiber reinforced gypsum (GFRG) walls of her Guangzhou Opera House in China (2003–10). Hadid carefully mapped the placement of the pattern on the shoe and spiraling strap to emphasize effects of fluid and continuous movement, as the pattern expands and contracts around the foot and leg while the wearer is in motion.

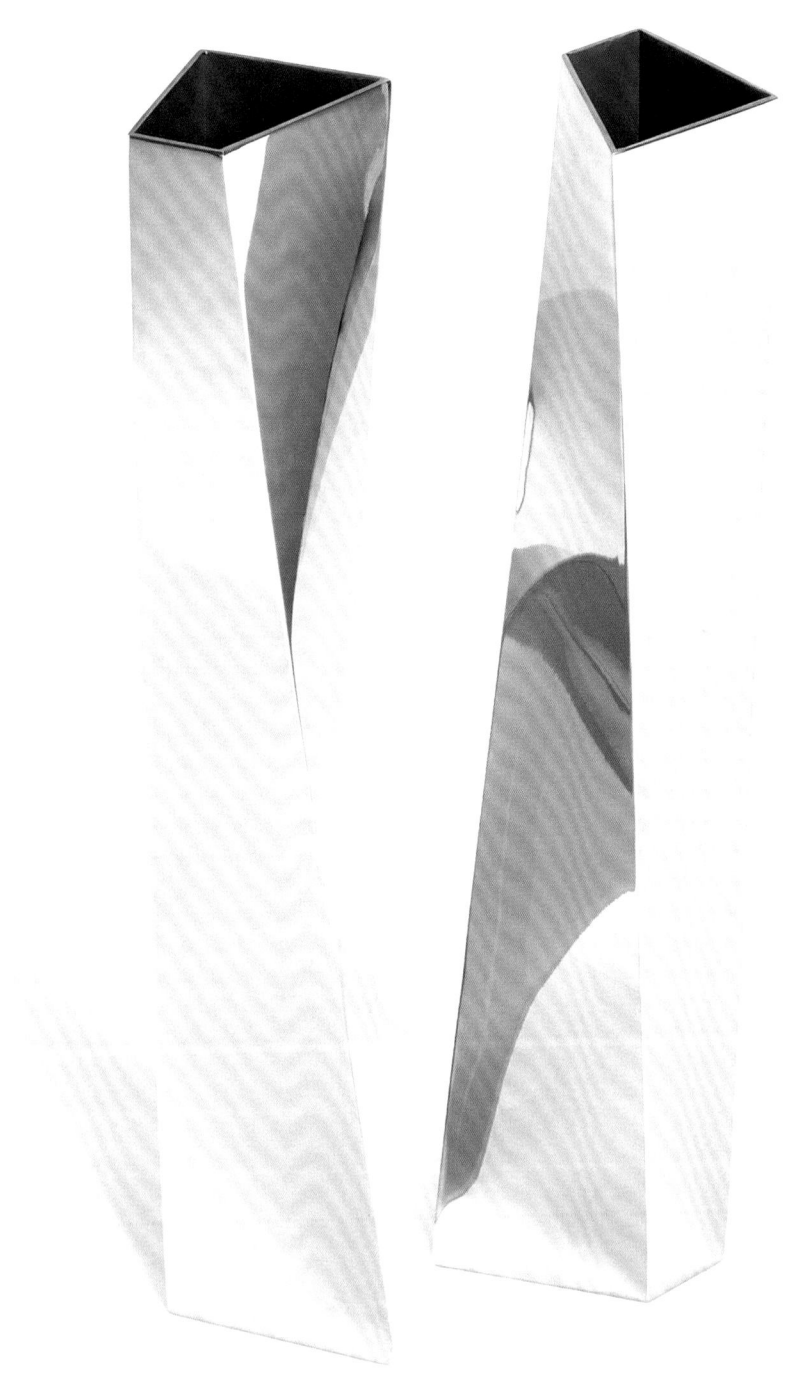

Cat. 19
Crevasse Vases | 2005
Made by Alessi S.p.A.
Stainless steel, PVD coating; H 16 9/16" (42 cm)
Silver: Philadelphia Museum of Art. Gift of Lisa S. Roberts, 2008-58-3 (left); lent by Alessi S.p.A. (right)
Gold: Lent by Alessi S.p.A.

In response to the World Trade Center disaster of 2001, innovative Italian metalware manufacturer Alberto Alessi (b. 1946) invited eight architects, including Zaha Hadid, to present large visionary study models of skyscrapers for ground zero (each built to a scale of 1/100) at the Eighth International Biennale of Architecture in Venice in 2002. Titled *City of Towers*, the exhibition, held in Venice's historic Arsenale, featured the towers designed by Hadid, who was simultaneously developing prototypes for Alessi's "Tea and Coffee Towers" project (2003). Her Biennale proposal evoked the original towers with a sinuous pair of twisting/merging double towers, a thinner pair for residential apartments and a thicker one for offices. The design was also published in a different context in *New York Magazine*, where architect and critic Joseph Giovannini described it as a reinvention of the "skyscraper as a building type, operating on the principle of connecting rather than isolating floors and people and varying spaces rather than repeating them identically."[1] *Crevasse* is a direct offspring of Hadid's *City of Towers* design; in fact, two prototype vases were exhibited in the plinth of the large model in Venice. Conceived as twinned towers, each pair of *Crevasse* vases is cut like the fissure the name suggests from a single block of stainless steel and scored along two diagonal lines at differing angles, creating a warped, inverted surface that appears to twist away from and merge with its twin at various points along the vertical axis. The vases are produced in mirror-polished stainless steel and with colored PVD coatings.

1. Joseph Giovannini, "Rising to Greatness," *New York Magazine*, September 16, 2002, http://nymag.com/news/articles/wtc/proposals/architects.

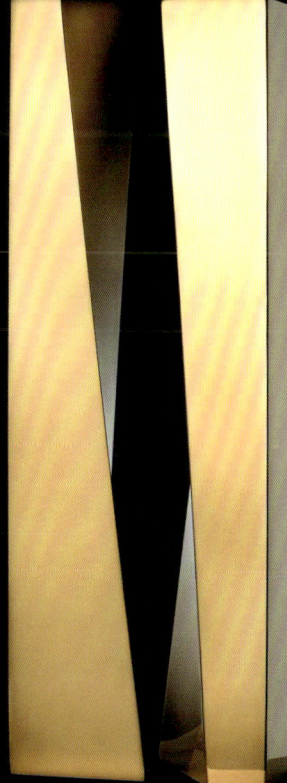

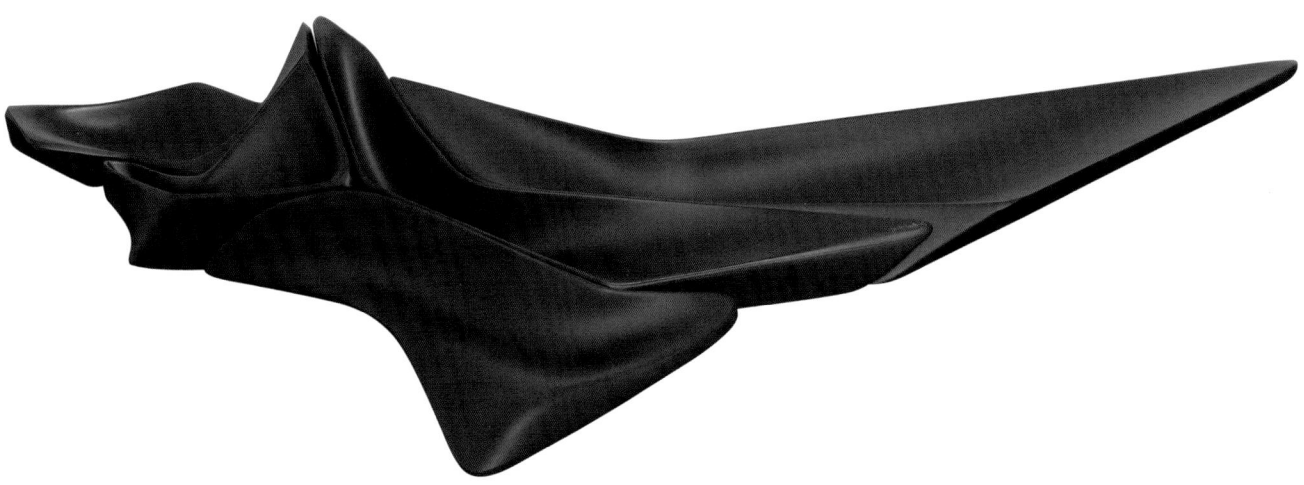

Cat. 20
***Niche* Centerpiece** | 2009
Made by Alessi S.p.A.
Black melamine with opaque finish, L 23 ⅝" (60 cm)
Philadelphia Museum of Art. Gift of Alessi, 2011-49-22a–e

Hadid's *Niche* centerpiece for Alessi is a functional table sculpture. Its five modular, black melamine elements, with depressions for food or display, can be assembled in multiple configurations, nesting to create solid forms or standing alone as distinct objects. The elements are defined by sloping planes whose corresponding profiles meet with the fluid, parallel movement of a landscape formation, like lava flows hardened into igneous rock. Exploring the possibilities of curvilinear geometry at different scales, the centerpiece shares formal elements with some of Hadid's architectural proposals—for example, the use of lateral connections to tie together the main longitudinal axis of an emergent hybrid system, as in the Kartal Pendik Masterplan for Istanbul (2006; fig. 11).

Fig. 11
Kartal Pendik Masterplan for Istanbul (2006)
Courtesy Zaha Hadid Architects, London

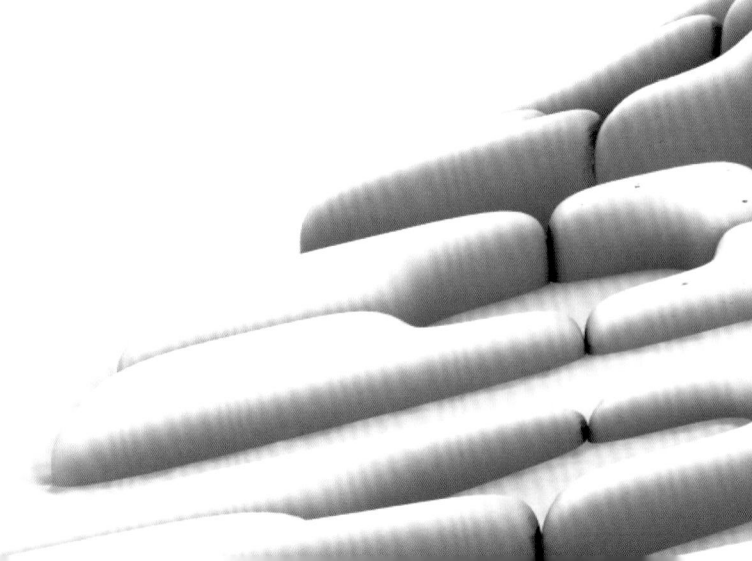

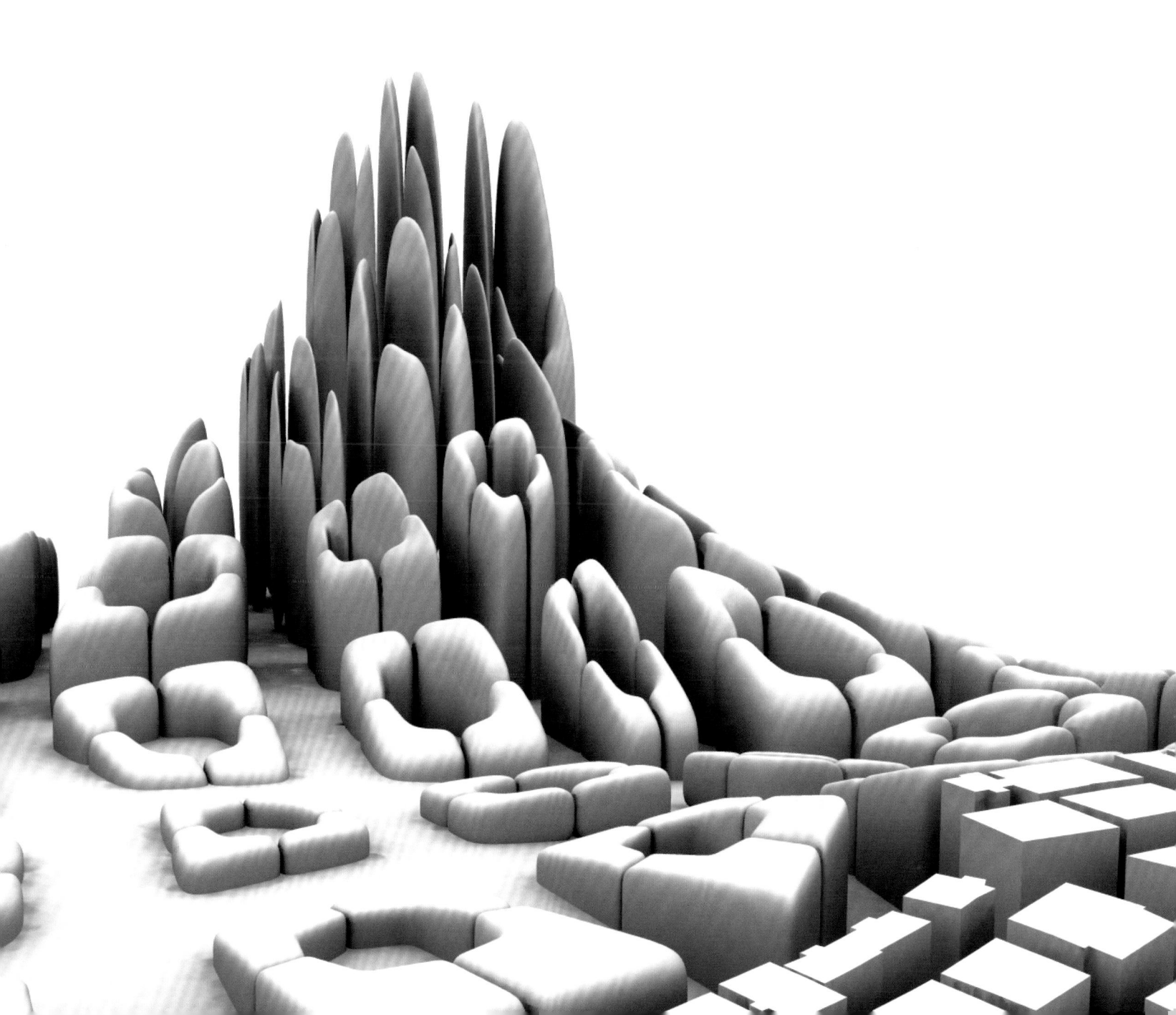

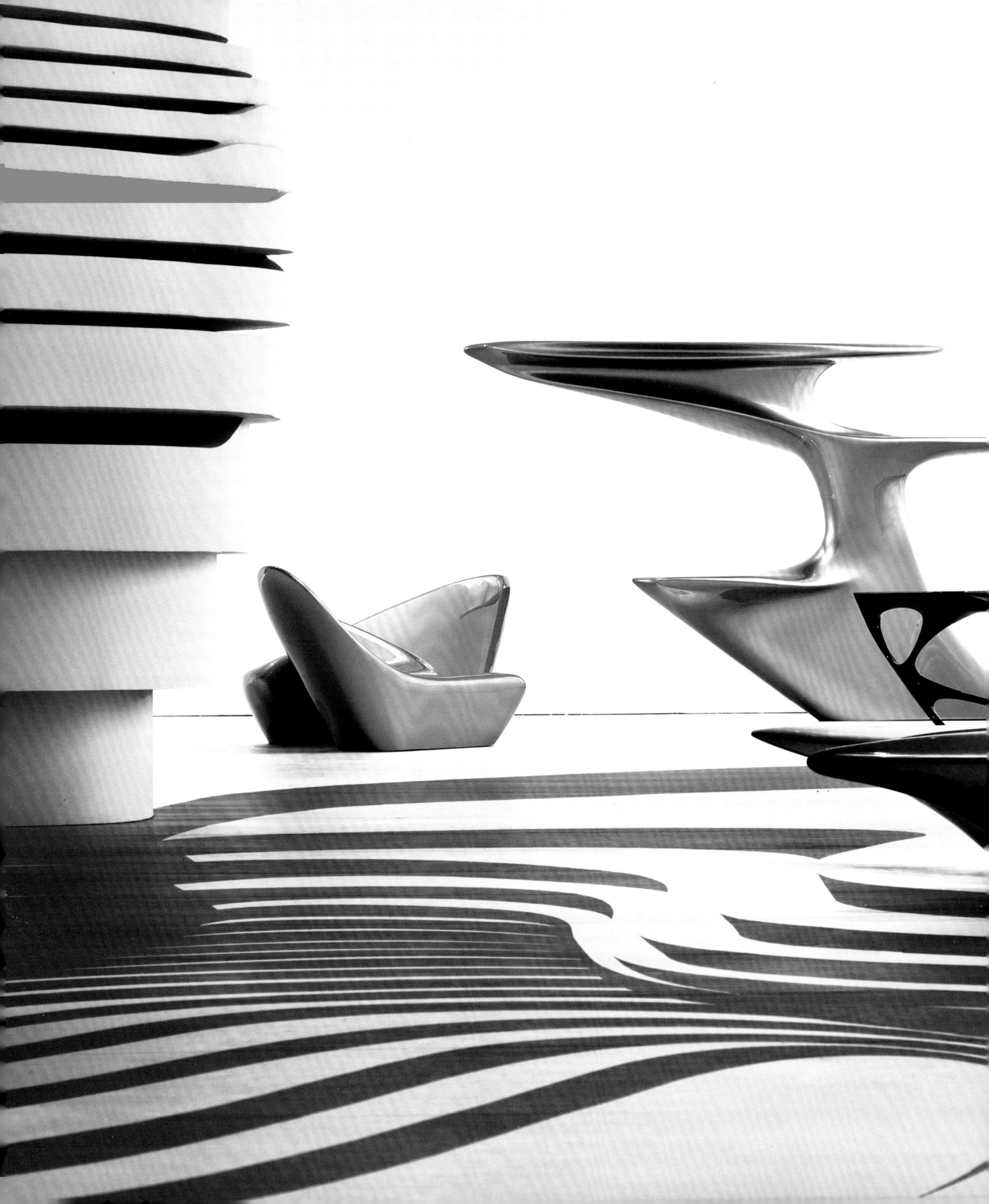

Exhibition Design

ZAHA HADID ARCHITECTS

Zaha Hadid: Form in Motion is the first exhibition in the United States to focus on Hadid's furniture and design objects in a site-specific environment designed by the architect and her firm, Zaha Hadid Architects (ZHA) of London. The exhibition presents an unprecedented look at the firm's innovations in process, collaboration, materials, and manufacturing. In doing so, it provides a means of exploring the impact of new technology on twenty-first-century architecture and design through Hadid's singular cross-disciplinary approach, in which the fields of architecture, urbanism, and design are closely linked.

The exhibition reflects ZHA's continued exploration of a new architectural language of fluidity that encompasses a broad range of design practices and project scales. Evolving from contemporary demands for increased complexity and variety, this new language is driven by the latest advances in computational design processes and fabrication technologies.

The all-encompassing exhibition environment of *Zaha Hadid: Form in Motion* transforms the gallery into a dynamic and fluid composition, demonstrating the architect's radical process of reinterpreting shared social settings for communication and interaction. A floor-to-ceiling undulating surface, fabricated from CNC-milled polystyrene, and tone-on-tone vinyl floor graphics fracture traditional rules of space and prescriptive notions of form, while Hadid's shifting perspectives pull the visitor into the environment to specific points of interaction and exchange. Crevices and rhythmic protrusions within the wavelike striated walls provide settings for the display of the studio's selected design products. This constant disorientation and reorientation of the visitor reveals the spatial complexity of Hadid's visionary creations, reinventing the balance between object and space. The video gallery environment behind the fluvial wall construct invites the visitor to discover a selection of Hadid's works through computer animations and still images of her architectural projects and design objects.

Checklist of the Exhibition

Cat. 1
Z-Play Seating Elements, 2002
Design: Zaha Hadid with Patrik Schumacher
Project Architect: Woody K.T. Yao
Design Team: Caroline Voet, Woody K.T. Yao, Chris Dopheide, Eddie Can, Maha Kutay, Melissa Woolford
Manufacturer: Sawaya & Moroni, Milan, 1984–present
Cold-foamed polyurethane, wool upholstery
Each piece 16 9/16 x 28 3/8 x 28 3/8" (42 x 72 x 72 cm)
Lender: Sawaya & Moroni

Cat. 2
Vortexx Chandeliers, 2005
Design: Zaha Hadid with Patrik Schumacher
Project Architect: Thomas Vietzke
Manufacturer: Zumtobel Lighting GmbH, Dornbirn, Austria, 1950–present, in collaboration with Sawaya & Moroni, Milan, 1984–present
Fiberglass, car paint, acrylic, LED
Black: 80 x 60 x 65" (203.2 x 152.4 x 165.1 cm)
White: 60 x 60 x 65" (152.4 x 152.4 x 165.1 cm)
Lender: Private collection

Cat. 3
Dune Formations Furniture Elements, 2007
Design: Zaha Hadid with Patrik Schumacher
Design Team: Michele Pasca di Magliano, Viviana Muscettola
Designed for David Gill Galleries, London, 1987–present
Aluminum (*Stardune 1, Stardune 3, Dune 02*); polyurethane resin, lacquer (all others)
Stardune 1 bench: 30 5/16 x 101 9/16 x 25 3/16" (77 x 258 x 64 cm)
Stardune 3 bench: 31 7/8 x 96 7/8 x 29 1/2" (81 x 246 x 75 cm)
Dune 02 shelf/desk: 14 9/16 x 137 x 28 3/8" (37 x 348 x 72 cm)
Dune 04 shelf: 3 15/16 x 137 x 22 13/16" (10 x 358 x 58 cm)
Dune 05 shelf: 3 9/16 x 157 7/16 x 30 11/16" (9 x 399 x 78 cm)
Dune 06 shelf: 4 5/16 x 133 7/16 x 30 5/16 inches (11 x 339 x 77 cm)
Dune A shelf: 20 1/16 x 149 3/16 x 20 1/16" (51 x 379 x 51 cm)
Dune B shelf: 20 1/2 x 114 3/16 x 31 1/8" (52 x 290 x 79 cm)
Dune E shelf: 19 11/16 x 145 11/16 x 16 9/16" (50 x 370 x 42 cm)
Dune Tree 1 shelves: 77 15/16 x 155 1/2 x 37 3/8" (198 x 395 x 95 cm)
Lender: David Gill Galleries

Cat. 4
Mesa Table, 2007
Design: Zaha Hadid with Patrik Schumacher
Project Designer: Saffet Kaya Bekiroglu
Design Team: Chikara Inamura, Melike Altinisik
Manufacturer: Vitra GmbH, Birsfelden, Switzerland, 1934–present
Polyurethane base, fiberglass top, metallic paint finish
27 9/16 x 159 7/16 x 64 15/16" (70 x 405 x 165 cm)
Lender: Vitra Design Museum, Weil am Rhein, Germany

Cat. 5
Crater Table, 2007
Design: Zaha Hadid with Patrik Schumacher
Project Designer: Saffet Kaya Bekiroglu
Design Team: Chikara Inamura, Chrysostomos Tsimourdagkas
Designed for David Gill Galleries, London, 1987–present
Aluminum with polished finish
11 13/16 x 29 1/2 x 104 3/4" (30 x 75 x 266 cm)
Lender: David Gill Galleries

Cat. 6
Moon System Sofa and Ottoman, 2007
Design: Zaha Hadid with Patrik Schumacher
Design Lead: Viviana Muscettola
Design Team: Michele Pasca di Magliano
Manufacturer: B&B Italia, Novedrate, Italy, 1966–present
Steel, cold-pressed polyurethane foam, nylon/polyurethane/spandex upholstery
Sofa: 33 7/16 x 113 3/8 x 78 3/4" (85 x 288 x 200 cm)
Ottoman: 11 13/16 x 59 7/16 x 42 1/2" (30 x 151 x 108 cm)
Lender: B&B Italia

Cat. 7
Kloris Seating Elements, 2008
Design: Zaha Hadid with Patrik Schumacher
Design Team: Melodie Leung, Tom Wuenschmann, Yael Brosiloski
Designed for and in collaboration with Julian A. Treger and Kenny Schachter / Rove Projects LLP, London, 2004–present
Glass-reinforced plastic with high-gloss lacquer finish, steel base plates
31 1/2 x 200 13/16 x 255 7/8" (80 x 510 x 650 cm)
Lender: Kenny Schachter / Rove Projects LLP

Cat. 8
Zephyr Sofa, 2010
Design: Zaha Hadid with Patrik Schumacher
Design Team: Fulvio Wirz, Mariagrazia Lanza, Maha Kutay
Designed for Zaha Hadid Architects, London, 1980–present
Lacquered fiberglass, polyurethane-coated polyester upholstery
28 3/4 x 111 7/8 x 104 3/8" (73 x 284 x 265 cm)
Lender: Zaha Hadid Architects

Cat. 9
Z-Chair, 2011
Design: Zaha Hadid with Patrik Schumacher
Design Team: Fulvio Wirz, Mariagrazia Lanza, Maha Kutay, Woody K.T. Yao
Manufacturer: Sawaya & Moroni, Milan, 1984–present
Stainless steel
34 5/8 x 36 1/4 x 24" (88 x 92 x 61 cm)
Lender: Sawaya & Moroni

Cat. 10
Tea and Coffee Service, 1995–96
Design: Zaha Hadid
Design Team: Maha Kutay, Anne Save de Beaurecueil
Manufacturer: Sawaya & Moroni, Milan, 1984–present
Silver
Teapot: 11 x 5 7/8 x 3 1/8" (28 x 15 x 8 cm)
Coffeepot: 11 x 3 15/16 x 3 9/16" (28 x 10 x 9 cm)
Milk jug: 7 7/8 x 3 9/16 x 2 3/4" (20 x 9 x 7 cm)
Sugar bowl: 3 15/16 x 3 9/16 x 2 3/4" (10 x 9 x 7 cm)
Lender: Sawaya & Moroni

Cat. 11
Z-Car I, 2005–6
Design: Zaha Hadid with Patrik Schumacher
Project Designer: Jens Borstelmann
Design Team: David Seeland
Designed for and in collaboration with Kenny Schachter / Rove Projects LLP, London, 2004–present
High-density polyurethane foam with pearlescent finish
66 15/16 x 149 5/8 x 70 7/8" (170 x 380 x 180 cm)
Lender: Kenny Schachter / Rove Projects LLP

Cat. 12
Flatware (2 sets), 2007
Design: Zaha Hadid with Patrik Schumacher
Project Designer: Jens Borstelmann
Manufacturer: WMF, Württembergische Metallwarenfabrik AG, Geislingen an der Steige, Germany, 1853–present
Stainless steel
Table fork: L 8 13/16" (22.4 cm)
Dessert fork: L 6 1/2" (16.6 cm)
Table knife: L 9 5/8" (24.5 cm)
Teaspoon: L 5 7/8" (14.9 cm)
Tablespoon: L 8 15/16" (22.7 cm)
Set 1: Philadelphia Museum of Art. Gift of Lisa S. Roberts, 2007-106-2–6
Set 2: Lender: Francine and Stuart Gerstein

Cat. 13
Fusital Door Handles, 2007
Design: Zaha Hadid with Patrik Schumacher
Design Architect: Woody K.T. Yao
Manufacturer: Valli & Valli, Milan, 1934–present
Brass, Nikrall Zamak alloy
Door handle: 2 5/8 x 6 3/4" (6.7 x 17.1 cm)
Door plate: 2 9/16 x 3/8" (6.5 x 1 cm)
Lender: Valli & Valli USA, a division of ASSA ABLOY

Cat. 14
Bowl, 2007
Design: Zaha Hadid with Patrik Schumacher
Design Lead: Saffet Kaya Bekiroglu
Design Team: Maha Kutay, Melissa Woolford, Tarek Shamma
Manufacturer: Sawaya & Moroni, Milan, 1984–present
Silver
5 1/8 x 23 5/8 x 10 13/16" (13 x 60 x 27.5 cm)
Lender: Sawaya & Moroni

Cat. 15
Glace Collection Jewelry, 2009
Design: Zaha Hadid with Patrik Schumacher
Design Team: Swati Sharma, Maria Araya
Manufacturer: Swarovski AG, Wattens, Austria, 1895–present
Colored resin, Swarovski crystals in jet and crystal
Necklace: 5 1/2 x 8 11/16" (14 x 22 cm)
Cuff 1: 1 15/16 x 4 1/8" (5 x 10.5 cm)
Cuff 2: 1 15/16 x 4 5/16" (5 x 11 cm)
Ring 1: 1 15/16 x 1 3/4" (4.9 x 4.5 cm)
Ring 2: 1 3/8 x 2 3/4" (3.5 x 7 cm)
Lender: Atelier Swarovski

Cat. 16
Celeste Necklace, 2008
Design: Zaha Hadid with Patrik Schumacher
Project Designer: Swati Sharma
Design Team: Kevin McClellan, Maha Kutay
Manufacturer: Swarovski AG, Wattens, Austria, 1895–present
Made with Swarovski gemstones in topaz white, smoky quartz, and black spinel; blackened silver
15 3/4 x 16 15/16" (40 x 43 cm)
Lender: Swarovski Runway Rocks

Cat. 17
Melissa Shoes, 2008
Design: Zaha Hadid with Patrik Schumacher
Project Director: Ana M. Cajiao
Design Team: Maria Araya, Muthahar Khan
Manufacturer: Grendene S.A., Farroupilha, Rio Grande do Sul, Brazil, 1971–present
Mold-injected plastic
Black (women's size 6): length 9" (22.9 cm)
Purple (women's size 9): length 10" (25.4 cm)
Lender: Melissa Shoes

Cat. 18
Zaha Hadid Limited Edition and Diffusion Edition Footwear for Men and Women, 2009
Design: Zaha Hadid with Patrik Schumacher
Project Director: Woody K.T. Yao
Design Lead: Maria Araya
Design Team: Danilo Arsic, Margarita Yordanova Valova, Maha Kutay, Nick Armitage, Dylan Davies
Manufacturer: Lacoste S.A., Paris, 1933–present
Leather, rubber
Various sizes
Lender: Lacoste Footwear

Cat. 19
Crevasse Vases, 2005
Design: Zaha Hadid with Patrik Schumacher
Design Team: Woody K.T. Yao, Thomas Vietzke
Manufacturer: Alessi S.p.A., Crusinallo, Italy, 1921–present
Silver: Stainless steel
Gold, brown, gunmetal: Stainless steel, PVD coating
16 9/16 x 2 3/8 x 3 1/8" (42 x 6 x 8 cm)
Silver: Philadelphia Museum of Art. Gift of Lisa S. Roberts, 2008-58-3
Gold, brown, gunmetal, silver: Lender: Alessi S.p.A.

Cat. 20
Niche Centerpieces (2 sets), 2009
Design: Zaha Hadid with Patrik Schumacher
Design Team: Woody K.T. Yao, Melodie Leung
Manufacturer: Alessi S.p.A., Crusinallo, Italy, 1921–present
Black melamine with opaque finish
2 3/4 x 23 5/8 x 11 13/16" (7 x 60 x 30 cm)
Set 1: Philadelphia Museum of Art. Gift of Alessi, 2011-49-22a–e
Set 2: Lender: Alessi S.p.A.

Zaha Hadid

KATHRYN HIGGINS

Zaha Hadid defines the iconoclast: a creative visionary who has challenged the conventions of her profession, achieving what others deemed impossible and building what others defined as unbuildable. From her earliest calligraphic brush strokes and mathematically precise paintings to the sweeping arcs and connective footprint of her new CMA CGM Headquarters skyscraper in Marseille, France (2005–11), Hadid's recasting of the relationship between object and field, private and public, and architect and client has kept her in the public consciousness for more than thirty years.

Often cited as the most prominent contemporary female architect, Hadid was born in Baghdad on October 31, 1950, and grew up in a well-educated, politically active family. Her father, Mohammed Hadid (1907–1999), an economist and graduate of the London School of Economics, was leader of the Iraqi National Democratic Party, which championed workers' rights, political reform, and the restoration of democratic processes, and served as a cabinet minister in the new republic. The youngest of three children, Zaha absorbed the varied skyline of Baghdad with its minarets and new modernist buildings. She was educated in convent schools in Baghdad and Switzerland and studied mathematics at the American University of Beirut in 1971 before moving to London to attend the Architectural Association School of Architecture (AA) from 1972 to 1977.

Undaunted by the underrepresentation of women in architecture, Hadid charted her own path under the tutelage of AA director Alvin Boyarski and professors Rem Koolhaas and Elia Zenghelis. Reflecting the emerging social and political consciousness of late-1960s Europe, the AA was an incubator of radical ideas challenging the notions of postmodern classicism. Following graduation, Hadid joined Koolhaas and Zenghelis's architectural firm, the Office for Metropolitan Architecture (OMA), leaving in 1980 to found Zaha Hadid Architects (ZHA), based in London. Throughout this period, she continued the revision of early Constructivism that she had begun at the AA. While her theoretically oriented neo-modernist contemporaries questioned modernism's edicts in written treatises, Hadid expressed her theories in visual form, on the canvas and drawing board. Her winning entry for The Peak (1983), an entertainment complex in Hong Kong, though never realized, conveyed the potentiality of dynamic, interconnected, naturally derived forms in motion in relation to program and site.

Hadid's focus on seamless architecture—a term both overused and underexplained in relation to her work—is at its core concerned with the connectivity of the parts to the whole, of the idea to the process as well as the product. Her career reveals a continuous spatial and cultural reflexivity, constantly anticipating the potential of form-making, social progress, and material construction, rather than relying upon familiar forms and practices. The introduction of advanced computer technology in the 1980s freed her designs from the canvas and drawing board, allowing greater expression of the continuity and spatial freedom firmly rooted in her practice. The rapid evolution of computer-aided design (CAD), its integration with building technology through parametric modeling, and the cross-pollination of materials from other disciplines (such as aeronautics, for the thermoformed double curvature panels on the Nordpark Railway Stations in Innsbruck, Austria; 2004–7) fulfilled her visions for free-form geometries that belie gravitational and social limits. Hadid's first building, the Vitra Fire Station in Weil am Rhein, Germany (1990–94), captured and redefined the surrounding context with a series of shifting concrete and glass planes suspended in a state of frozen movement. ZHA's technical progress and transition toward the conceptual and physical fluidity of space is revealed in Hadid's recently completed MAXXI—Museo Nazionale delle Arti del XXI Secolo in Rome (2010), which replaces the traditional object-based promenade of the museum experience with pathways that create a multiplicity of views and relationships internally while reflecting and capturing the surrounding flows of urban life. Global in reach, programmatically and formally varied, the firm is currently completing the London 2012 Olympic Aquatics Centre and CMA CGM skyscraper (Hadid's first). While her architectural projects continue to push the limits of engineering and current building technologies, Hadid's parallel design practice, the subject of this book and exhibition, has become a forum for experimentation and realization of biomorphic objects that are seamless, spatially continuous, and abstractly familiar.

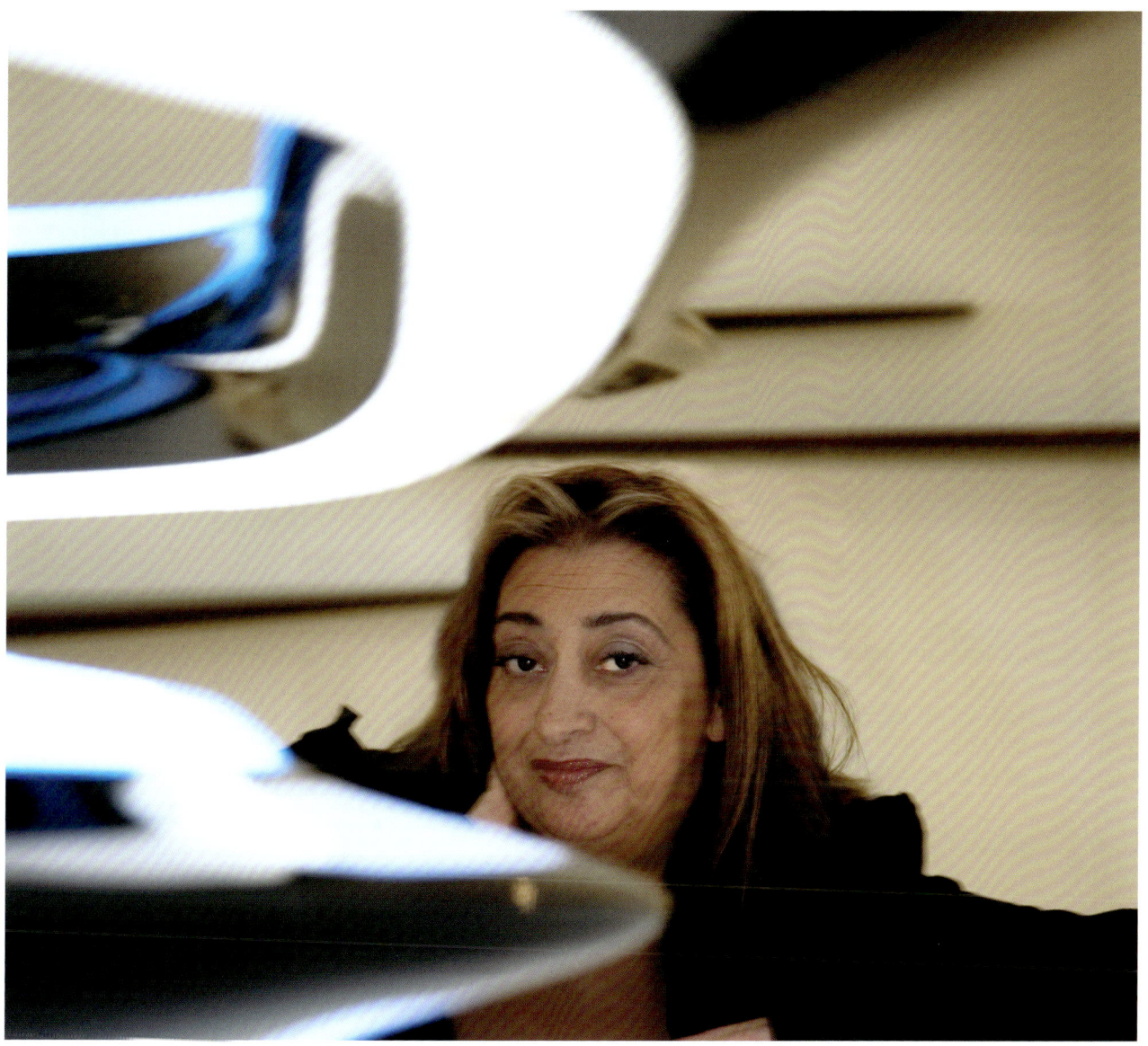

Throughout her career, Hadid has viewed teaching as an invaluable component of her practice. Currently a professor at the University of Applied Arts Vienna, she has previously held teaching positions at the AA; the Graduate School of Design, Harvard University; and the School of Architecture at the University of Illinois–Chicago. She has also been a guest professor at the Hochschule für Bildende Künste in Hamburg; the Graduate School of Architecture, Planning and Preservation at Columbia University; and the Knowlton School of Architecture at the Ohio State University; as well as the Eero Saarinen Visiting Professor of Architectural Design at the Yale School of Architecture. Recently named one of Newsweek magazine's "150 Women Who Shake the World," Hadid's unique style and architectural practice have been recognized since the beginning of her career, when she was awarded the AA's Diploma Prize in 1977. Hadid is an honorary member of the American Academy of Arts and Letters, an honorary Fellow of the American Institute of Architects, and Commander of the Order of the British Empire (CBE). In 2004, she won architecture's highest award: the Pritzker Architecture Prize. Most recently, in 2010 Hadid was awarded the Royal Institute of British Architects Stirling Prize for MAXXI.

Glossary
KATHRYN HIGGINS

biomorphic – A nonrepresentational form or pattern that resembles a living organism in shape or appearance. In art, biomorphic forms or images are those that, while abstract, nevertheless refer to or evoke plants, animals, or human beings.

carbon-fiber-reinforced polymers (CFRP) or carbon-fiber-reinforced plastics (CRP) – Commonly referred to as "carbon fiber," this lightweight, durable composite material, originally developed for the aeronautic and auto industries, is made from a variety of polymers, including epoxy resin. Unidirectional layers of woven fibers are placed into a thermoforming mold and heated to temperatures exceeding 600°F before curing. Offering the same tensile strength as steel at a quarter of the weight, carbon fiber can be custom-fabricated with the woven fibers placed in a direction that increases the strength at a specific location in a particular application.

computer-aided design (CAD) – The use of computer technology for precision drafting, design documentation, and manufacturing. CAD software can be used to create two-dimensional drawings or three-dimensional models and photorealistic images, called "renderings," for use in fields such as architecture, engineering, and manufacturing.

computer numerical control (CNC) – Advanced manufacturing technology that allows for the automation of machining tools, such as milling machines, lathes, and injection molding, operated by computer-aided manufacturing programs (CAM) and CAD files. This rapid-prototyping technology utilizes CAD/CAM software to generate G-code, or specific action-coded instructions for the machine to perform, which then translates two-dimensional profiles or three-dimensional solid/surface geometry into machined products.

ethyl vinyl acetate (EVA) – Popularly known as foam rubber, EVA is a nontoxic foam copolymer produced from the combination of ethylene and vinyl acetate and used predominantly as cushioning in running shoes.

glass fiber reinforced gypsum (GFRG) – A noncombustible composite panel used exclusively for interior applications, GFRG consists of high-strength glass fiber embedded in a mixture of raw gypsum and cement. Lightweight, durable, and nontoxic, GFRG can be custom-manufactured in a variety of shapes and finishes, offering reduced costs and weight.

injection molding – A manufacturing process in which a thermoplastic or thermosetting plastic material is fed into a heated barrel, mixed, and forced into a machined mold, where it cools and hardens. Used to produce items ranging from plastic chairs to shoes to body panels for cars.

non-uniform rational basis splines (NURBS) – Mathematical representations of three-dimensional geometry used in computer graphics to accurately describe and generate both standard geometric objects such as lines and circles and free-form geometry such as complex surfaces and solids. Highly flexible and accurate, NURBS-based modeling reduces the file size required to represent a piece of geometry over common polygonal (faceted) approximations while producing smooth, seamless surfaces. NURBS tools are found in various three-dimensional modeling and animation software packages such as Form Z, Maya, 3ds Max, and RhinoCAD.

parametric modeling – Often referred to as feature-based modeling, parametric modeling utilizes the computer to design objects by modeling their components with real-world behaviors and attributes. In a parametric modeling program, the characteristics of each component, defined by specific parameters and relationships, are interdependent with all other components so that an alteration to one component results in the automated adjustment of all others in relation to the first.

polyurethane (PUR or PU) – Any polymer composed of a chain of organic units joined by carbamate (urethane) links. Examples of current polyurethane use include flexible-yet-resilient foam seating and rigid foam insulation panels.

physical vapor deposition (PVD) – A group of vacuum coating techniques used to deposit thin film coatings that enhance the properties and performance of tools and machine components. PVD optical coatings provide solar control to windows; ceramic coatings increase surface wear on watches; and low-friction coatings reduce energy loss and lubricant needs in racecars.

polyvinyl chloride (PVC) – A common thermoplastic resin used in a variety of manufactured products, including rainwear, footwear, construction pipes, windows, and doorframes. PVC is currently the third most widely produced plastic worldwide.

rapid prototyping – An additive modeling method in which an object is created from a CAD drawing that has been processed to create one or more files of the object "sliced" into layers. The CAD file is input into the software controlling the rapid prototyping machine, which then calculates, duplicates, and cuts the profile and area of each layer. Conversely, CNC machining utilizes a subtractive method, cutting away at a solid block of material to create the final object.

tectonic – From the Greek *tektonikós*, pertaining to the art or science of construction. In geology, of or relating to the structure of the earth's crust and/or the forces or conditions within the earth that cause movements of the crust.

thermoforming – A manufacturing process in which a plastic resin sheet or "film" is heated to a pliable temperature, formed to a desired shape in a pressure- or vacuum-assisted mold, and trimmed to create a usable product.